STEP-BY-STEP
CAKE
DECORATING
with CHERYLSHUEN

STEP-BY-STEP
CAKE
DECORATING
with CHERYLSHUEN

KOK PEI SHUEN

Marshall Cavendish
Cuisine

Your sharing enriches my journey of learning.
Especially for you, Teachers in my life.

CONTENTS

Acknowledgements

I would like to thank my mama,
Mok Wai Pheng, who has always led a very
humble life and never ceased in her effort to
ensure all her children received good education.
To my dad, Kok Kai Choong, who is always very
encouraging and supportive of my ventures,
thank you for your unconditional love.

Thank you my sweetheart, Chun Ying,
for being my great inspiration. Your arrival
prompted me to embark on a journey of
baking cakes for children. Julie, thank you
for being supportive always, I'm grateful
for your contributions.

I would like to express my gratitude to many
people who saw me through this book. Thank
you for your patience and kind assistance.
Thank you Lydia Leong, for extending this
opportunity to me. I am grateful to Audrey Yow,
Adithi Khandadi, Liu Hongde, Chong Wen Fuh,
Vincent Chun Yong Hua, Leong Wing Keong and
Tjon Meilyn Lena for your contributions. I beg
forgiveness from all who have been with me
over the years, but whose names I have failed
to mention.

Every cake
tells a dream.

Introduction

Receiving the invitation to write a cake decorating book is one of the most incredible happenings in my journey of baking. It reminded me of my first encounter that led me to venture into the beautiful world of cake decorating. It reminded me of the very first cake decorating book that I still keep and treasure, the countless nights of practice and all the remarkable designs that I made, which brought me all the way to writing this book.

I am making this book useful for those who wish to bake and decorate like a professional. It is structured in an organised manner, and even a novice will not find it difficult to attempt cake decorating. All the fundamental skills and techniques will be covered under the section Preparing Cakes for Decoration. Following that will be an exciting discovery of how to apply these skills on the 20 amazing cake decorating projects, which were specially designed to bring the most practical and interesting experience to you.

Set yourself onto a comfortable armchair and prepare to immerse into the wonderful world of cake decorating!

Kok Pei Shuen
郭珮璇

Butter Cake *the basics*

140g Vegetable shortening
160g Fine sugar (a) 180 grams
260g Cake flour
½ tsp Salt
4 tsp Baking powder
240ml Milk
Juice Egg white 5 *eggs*
60g Fine sugar (b)

Steps:
preheat oven to 160 deg C
shortening till creamy, light
sugar (a) to (1)
salt, baking powder together
ternately to shortening mixture, start and end with flour
egg white until stiff and shiny, fold into flour
of 9inch round pan. Baking time
comes out clean
amount

How to Use This Book

Go through the section on Equipment and Tools to get familiar with some of the most essential tools for cake decorating. All items are briefly described to give you an idea of how to use these tools.

Important basics are group under the section Preparing Cakes for Decoration, which gives a straightforward description of the essential steps before starting on your project, such as preparing iced cakes and supporting the weight of cake tiers.

The section Cake and Icing Recipes contain various ideas for the base cakes, creams and icings, which you are free to experiment with to create your desired cake. All recipes have been tried and tested, so feel free to mix and match any combination to create your very own flavours.

Each of the 20 cake projects introduces the application of various techniques, and you will be guided by step-by-step pictures where necessary.

Here's wishing you a sweet cake journey!

Equipment and Tools

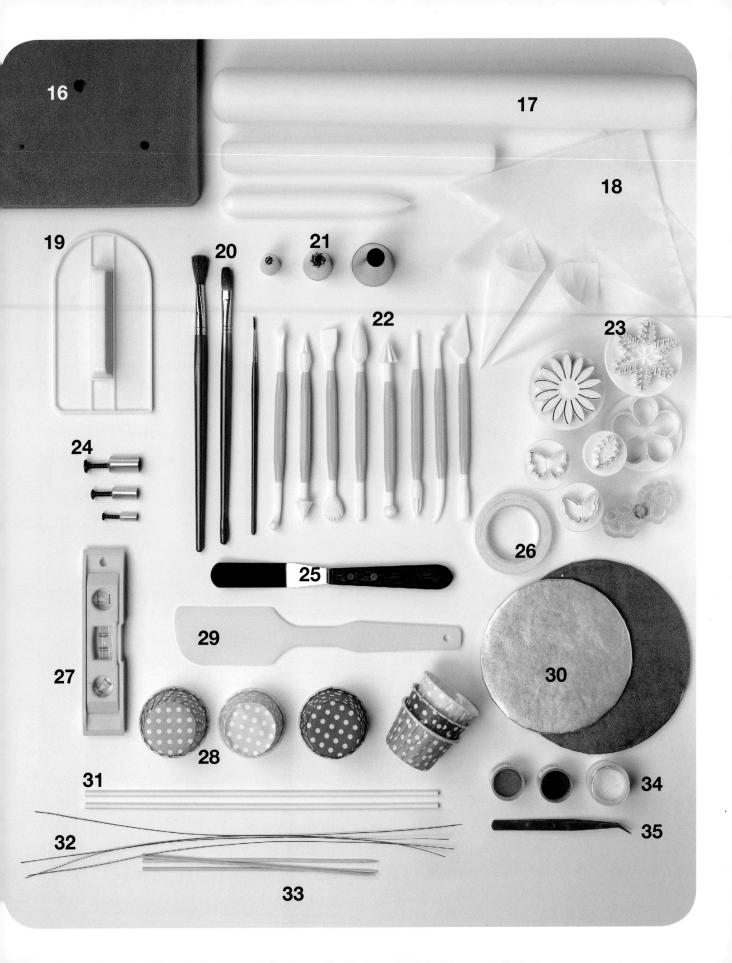

1 Wire Rack

A raised wire rack is essential for cooling freshly baked cakes. Its design allows air circulation, which cools cakes down evenly and prevents condensation from forming.

2 Parchment paper

Used to line baking trays and cake pans, parchment paper is a convenient way to prevent cakes from sticking to the pan. It is non-stick, heat-resistant and disposable. Some bakers prefer to grease the cake pan with butter or shortening before lining it with parchment paper, as the grease will hold the parchment paper in place as the batter is poured into the pan.

3 Baking tray

This is a handy tool with a variety of uses. While its main purpose is to hold food that is baking in the oven, such as cakes, breads and cookies, it is also good for organising ingredients like fondant and flower paste. Also, when dusting a cake, the tray can be placed underneath to collect loose powder or grains.

4 Sieve

The sieve is essentially used to remove lumps from dry ingredients that tend to clump, like flours and sugars. Sifting makes mixing easier and creates a smoother batter. It also ensures that the ingredients are evenly distributed.

5 Tiltable turntable

The turntable allows you to rotate the cake as you work on it, making decoration work easier and more convenient. To decorate different parts of the cake, choose the most comfortable tilting angle to reach the sides or bottom more easily. See the turntable in use on page 29.

6 Pastry mixer attachments

An electric pastry mixer is a handy equipment that usually comes with three types of attachments. The whisk (6a) is for whipping light materials like creams, the paddle (6b) is for mixing batter and the dough hook (6c) is for kneading dough.

7 Ruler

A ruler will come in useful while levelling cakes and measuring decorative items. It is also useful when required to cut straight.

8 Spatula

This is a silicone spatula, which is for stirring cake mixes.

9 Serrated knife

This is very good for slicing cakes into layers without causing it to misshapen or compress.

10 Tapered offset spatula

Its angled blade is useful for spreading and smoothening creamy ingredients onto cakes. The tapered end helps to reach narrow places.

11 Rotary cutter

A rotary cutter is useful when you need to create decorative patterns from fondant or flower paste. It glides easily and is very easy to use. To create wavy lines, use a rotary cutter with serrated edges.

12 Pastry brush

This is used for greasing cake pans or brushing jam over cake boards. A silicone pastry brush is particularly handy, as it can also be used to brush over delicate pastry. It is also easy to clean.

13 Measuring spoons

Measuring spoons are good for measuring small quantities precisely. The set pictured here includes $1/8$ tsp, $1/4$ tsp, $1/2$ tsp, 1 tsp and 1 Tbsp.

14 Round cutters

Round cutters of various sizes are used to cut out rounds of fondant or flower paste for decorating purposes.

15 Cake pans

These cake pans are made of stainless steel. To create a different size for each cake tier, use cake pans of different sizes.

16 Foam pad

The foam pad is used to thin out or shape fondant and flower paste, especially when creating flower petals.

17 Rolling pins

Available in different sizes, rolling pins are used for different purposes, like rolling out fondant and flower paste, and draping fondant over a cake. For shaping or rolling out smaller items, use a small rolling pin.

18 Piping bags

Small piping bags are good for the finer details of decorating. They are easily available in stores, or you can fold a simple piping bag from a small piece of parchment paper.

19 Fondant smoother

To achieve a smooth finishing for iced cakes, the fondant smoother is used to even out the fondant after it is applied to the cake.

20 Paintbrushes

Paintbrushes are used to colour decorations. They can be used on fondant and flower paste. A paintbrush is also good for brushing water or royal icing on items that need to be adhered to each other.

21 Piping tips

Different piping tips will create different shapes of buttercream or royal icing as it is being piped onto the cake. Choose the appropriate tip depending on how you want to decorate your cakes.

22 Fondant and flower paste tools

These tools are used to create desired shapes and patterns on fondant and flower paste. Each of them have dual ends for different purposes. Note that not all store-bought tools have the same dual ends as those pictured here. For example, the flower-shaper tool does not necessarily come with the bone tool at the other end. From left to right:

The flower-shaper and bone tool: The back of the flower-shaper tool (top end) is used for smoothing out petals or creating wide-shaped veining on flowers and leaves. The bone tool at the other end is used for thinning out edges of flowers or leaves to create realistic frilled edges. It can also be used to create round hollows in fondant or flower paste shapes, such as figurines.

The 5-star and tapered cone tool: The 5-star tool (top end) is used to impress star shapes or to create flower centres. It is also used as petal dividers and for creating textures and details. The tapered cone tool at the other end is for creating dents or hollows, such as those in fruits, like the tops of pears and apples.

The comb and shell tool: The comb tool (top end) is for impressing serrated patterns such as stitching on clothing or hair. The shell tool at the other end creates shell patterns and also paw-like patterns on the feet of animals.

The bulbous double-ended tool: Both the bulbous cone tool (top end) and the narrower tool at the other end is similar to the bone tool, as they are also ideal for creating frills for the edges of flower petals and leaves.

The serrated cone and ball tool: The serrated cone tool (top end) works like a tapered cone tool, and is great for shaping fruits. The ball tool at the other end is similar to the bone tool, and can also be used to shape petals, leaves and frills.

The ball and 6-star tool: The ball tool (top end) is smaller than the one mentioned above, and can be used for smaller items to achieve the same effect of the larger ball tool. The 6-star tool at the other end works like the 5-star tool.

The bone and leaf-shaper tool: The bone tool (top end) is smaller than the one mentioned above, and can be used for smaller items to achieve a similar effect. The leaf-shaper tool at the other end is for creating finer details like the veins on leaves or fine lines on other items.

The blade and scallop tool: The blade tool (top end) is useful for cutting and trimming. The scallop tool at the other end is great for creating facial features like smiling or frowning mouths, eyebrows and ears.

23 Cutters and presses

These come in various shapes and sizes, such as flowers, leaves and animals. They can be used to create decorations from fondant or flower paste. Press onto a sheet of fondant or flower paste, then gently release the decorative cutout for use.

24 Plunger cutters

Plunger cutters come in various shapes and designs, and are used to cut, emboss or press out fondant or flower paste decorations. To use, press onto a sheet of fondant or flower paste to imprint the design, then release the plunger.

25 Offset spatula

An offset spatula has an angled blade, which is useful for spreading and smoothening creamy ingredients onto cakes.

26 Florist tape

Available in different widths and colours, florist tape holds the stems of sugar flowers together. It can also be used to cover the wire stems of sugar flowers.

27 Spirit level

This tool is for ensuring that the cakes are level, which is important especially when putting together tiered cakes.

28 Cupcake liners

Apart from holding batter, the fancier cupcake liners let you decorate your cupcakes to your liking. If you have baked your cupcakes in plain liners, simply place the cupcakes into patterned liners without removing the plain ones.

29 Rubber spatula

Like the silicone spatula above, it can mix, spread or scrape batters and creams. Because it has a flat, flexible rubber head, it can reach difficult spaces. A rubber spatula is also less likely to scratch mixing bowls and other surfaces.

30 Cake boards

Available in different colours and sizes, cake boards are typically round or square. Choose the appropriate cake boards according to your cake sizes and designs.

31 Dowels

Dowels are used to support the weight of tiered cakes. They are generally made of plastic or wood, and can be trimmed according to the height of the cakes.

32 Wires

These metal wires are thin and flexible, and are used to make flower stems or other decorations to be inserted into the cakes.

33 Bamboo skewers or toothpicks

The ones pictured are bamboo skewers. These are useful for attaching pieces of fondant or flower paste together. For smaller items, toothpicks will suffice. For example, insert a toothpick into the torso of a figurine, then gently press the head into the toothpick until it joins with the torso.

34 Edible dusts

Edible dusts can be used to colour fondant or flower paste decorations. Before painting, mix the dust with clear liquor or water first. To give a shimmer, use lustre or pearl dusts.

35 Tweezers

A pair of tweezers is handy when arranging small decorative items.

Preparing Cakes
for Decoration

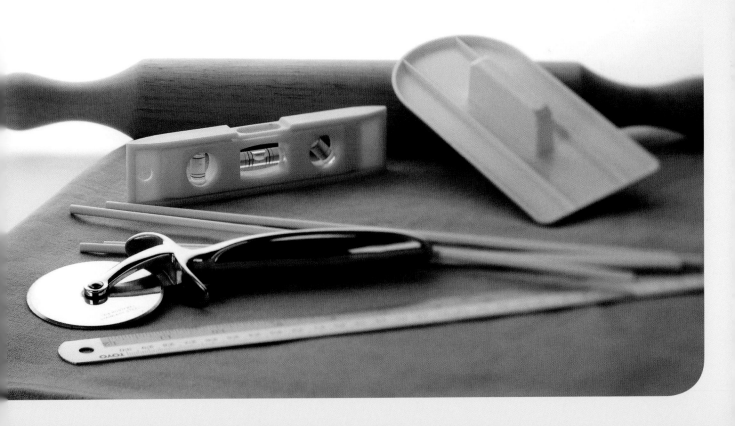

There are some basic preparations that should be done prior to decorating a cake. These handy icing techniques will give the cake a flat, smooth surface, making it a perfect backdrop for decoration. To ice a cake or cake board is to coat it with icing. The types of icing include sweet creamy spreads, such as buttercream and ganache, or fondant, a sweet doughy sugar paste.

A. ICING THE CAKE BOARD

This is the foundation of a cake, so it is important for it to be smooth and level. An iced cake board can be decorated too if desired.

Equipment and Ingredients:

- Brush
- Apricot jam
- Cake board
- Rolling pin
- Fondant
- Fondant smoother
- Small sharp knife

1. Brush a thin, even layer of apricot jam over cake board. Roll out fondant until about 3 mm ($^1/_8$ in) thick, then apply over cake board.

A1

2. Smooth fondant over cake board with a fondant smoother.

A2

3. Trim away excess with a sharp knife. Iced cake board is ready for use.

A3

B. LEVELLING

Before icing the cake, it must first be level, especially if making tiered cakes.

Equipment and Ingredients:

- Cake
- Ruler
- Serrated knife

1. Level the cake by trimming off the crust. Use a ruler to ensure it will be the same height all around. To make trimming easier, chill cake for 30–45 minutes beforehand.

B1

2. Halve the cake horizontally, cutting them into two layers, each about 2.5 cm (1 in) thick. If the cake is deep, divide into one or two more layers if desired.

C. FILLING AND COATING

The next step is to fill and coat the cake, which not only adds flavour, but also gives a smooth and even surface for icing the cake with fondant.

Equipment and Ingredients:

- Cake layers
- Cake board, not iced, same size as the base of the cake
- Buttercream or chocolate ganache
- Offset spatula
- Spirit level

1. Attach the first cake layer to a cake board with buttercream or chocolate ganache. This facilitates moving the cake later on without ruining the icing.

C2

C3

2. Using an offset spatula, spread an even coat of buttercream or chocolate ganache on one half of the cake.

3. Gently place the second half of the cake on top, and coat entire cake with buttercream or chocolate ganache, then smooth it out until the cake is level. If you require a higher cake, stack more layers before coating the entire cake.

4. Use a spirit level to check that the cake is level. Coat with more buttercream to level out the cake surface if necessary.

D. ICING WITH FONDANT

Covering a cake with fondant gives it a smooth finish, providing an ideal base for decorations.

Equipment and Ingredients:

- Rolling pin
- Fondant
- Filled and coated cake
- Fondant smoother
- Sharp knife or cutter
- Clean sharp pin
- Royal icing
- Iced cake board

1. Roll out fondant until about 5 mm ($^1/_4$ in) thick, or thinner if you prefer. It should be big enough to cover the cake, with some allowance of about 5 cm (2 in) all around. Drape fondant over a rolling pin and lay it over the cake.

D1

2. Using a fondant smoother, smooth over the top surface first before moving downwards to smoothen the side.

3. Once fondant is attached to the cake, trim away excess with a sharp knife or cutter. If any air bubbles form under the fondant, gently prick with a clean, sharp pin to remove the air, then smooth over with a fondant smoother.

4. Spread some royal icing onto the centre of the iced cake board prepared in Section A. Gently place iced cake onto the cake board. If assembling a tiered cake, skip this step and continue to Section E.

E. ASSEMBLING TIERED CAKES

After icing each of the cake tiers, they can now be assembled to make a tiered cake. The tiers are held stable with dowels. The dowels used here are plastic rods that support the weight of the higher tiers and prevent them from sinking into the cakes below.

Equipment and Ingredients:

- Royal icing
- Iced cake board
- Iced cake tiers
- Cake boards the size of higher tiers
- Toothpick
- Dowels
- Sharp knife or cutter

1. Spread some royal icing onto iced cake board and secure the first cake tier onto the centre of the board.

2. Pick a cake board the size of the next tier. Place on top of the first tier where the next tier will sit. Using the cake board as a guide, mark the spot by scoring on the first tier with a toothpick. Mark five spots centrally within the scored marking, where the dowels will be inserted.

3. Insert a dowel all the way down into the centre of the cake. Using a knife, mark the height of the cake on the dowel. Remove dowel from cake and trim away excess with a sharp knife. Trim the remaining dowels in this manner.

E3

4. Insert dowels into marked spots after trimming.

E4

5. Spread some royal icing on the centre of the cake. Gently place the next tier on top, using the scored mark as a guide.

E5

6. Repeat the steps above for the next tier.

DECORATING PROJECTS

Spring Wedding Bliss

Equipment

- Rolling pin
- Floral motif press
- Paintbrush
- Floral wires
- Wire clipper
- Styrofoam pad
- Hydrangea- or four-petal flower cutter
- Foam pad
- Bone tool
- Rack
- Five-petal flower cutters of various shapes and sizes
- Calla lily or heart-shape cutter

Ingredients

- Three square cake tiers of different sizes
- Fondant — white, light yellow
- Edible pearl dust — white
- Water
- Flower paste — lemon-yellow, purple, green and orange

METHOD

1. Prepare for decoration, following instructions in Sections A–D on pages 26–31.

    a. Use light yellow fondant to cover each tier.

2. Decorate edges of cake tiers with white floral motifs.

    a. Roll out white fondant until about 2 mm ($^1/_8$ in) thick.

    b. Dust floral motif press with white pearl dust, shake to remove excess, then press onto fondant to form floral motifs. Repeat until there are enough floral motifs to decorate all the cake tiers.

    c. Brush the underside of flower motifs with a little water and adhere onto cake edges. Repeat until all three tiers are decorated.

3. Assemble cake tiers. See instructions in Section E on pages 32–33.

4. Prepare flower stems.

4b

a. Cut enough floral wires for any number of flowers you wish to add. The stems should be about 10 cm (4 in) long, except for calla lilies, which should have 12.5-cm (5-in) stems.

b. Use a wire clipper to bend one end of each wire to form a hook. Set aside.

5. Form stems with flower centres.

5a

5c

a. For the hydrangeas, lightly dampen the hooked end of a wire, then press it into a small ball of lemon-yellow flower paste. Pinch to seal the opening so that the flower paste is secured over the hooked end. Repeat until flower centres for hydrangeas are done. Leave to dry overnight on a Styrofoam pad.

b. For the roses, ranunculus and calla lilies, roll some flower paste into a ball. Use lemon-yellow for roses and calla lilies, and purple for ranunculus flowers.

c. Dip the hooked end of a wire into some water, shake off excess and push the unhooked end through the ball. Gently pull the ball of flower paste towards the hooked end. Shape flower paste until one-third of it covers the hooked end. Pinch flower paste to make a pointed tip at the top, then shape the lower end to secure it over the wire. You should get a teardrop shape of flower paste, with the wire protruding from the rounder end.

d. Repeat to make flower centres for roses, calla lilies and ranunculus flowers. Make bigger centres to form larger roses if desired. Leave to dry overnight on a Styrofoam pad.

6. Form green hydrangeas.

6b

6c

6d

a. Roll out green flower paste thinly.

b. Press out petals using a hydrangea- or four-petal flower cutter.

c. On a foam pad, thin out edges with a bone tool to shape hydrangea petals.

d Insert a hydrangea stem down the centre of flower cutout. Gently overlap each petal slightly, forming a cup around the centre.

e. Repeat until desired number of hydrangeas are formed.

f. Hook hydrangeas upside down on a rack. Leave to dry overnight.

7. Form yellow roses.

7b–c

7e

7g

7h

a. Roll out lemon-yellow flower paste thinly.

b. Using five-petal flower cutters of the same shape but different sizes, press out flower shapes. Use progressively larger flower cutters for petals further out from the centre.

c. Place flower cutout centrally over one hole on a foam pad. Thin out edges with a bone tool to shape rose petals.

d. Holding up the foam pad, insert a rose stem down the centre of the shaped cutout. Use a larger rose centre for a bigger rose. When the base of the flower centre touches the cutout, hold onto the stem and carefully flip foam pad upside down. Push stem down and remove from the foam pad, holding onto the stem at the base of the flower centre with the other hand.

e. Wrap the flower cutout around the core, gently shaping some of the petals until they curve outwards to resemble rose petals.

f. Repeat to add as many layers as desired, until rose is of a desired size.

g. For the outermost petal, thin out the edges of the largest flower cutout, then pinch the tips of the petals.

h. Insert the stem with the half-formed rose into the centre of the cutout. Remove from foam pad in the same way as in Step 7d. Shape rose petals, gently curling out the edges.

i. Hook roses upside down on a rack. Leave to dry overnight.

8. Form purple ranunculus flowers.

8c

8d

8e

a. Roll out purple flower paste until about 2 mm ($^1/_8$ in) thick.

b. Using five-petal flower cutters of the same shape but different sizes, press out flower shapes. Use progressively larger flower cutters for petals further out from the centre.

c. Place flower cutout centrally over one hole on a foam pad. Starting from the base of each petal, use a bone tool to gently press and move in circular motions until the outer edges curl up.

d. Insert a ranunculus stem down the centre of the shaped cutout. Remove from foam pad in the same way as in Step 7d.

e. Gently overlap the petals with one another until it wraps around the centre.

f. Repeat to add layers of petals until each ranunculus is of a desired size.

g. Hook ranunculus flowers upside down on a rack. Leave to dry overnight.

9. Form orange calla lilies.

9b–c

9e

a. Roll out orange flower paste thinly.

b. Use a calla lily cutter to press out petals. If a calla lily cutter is unavailable, use a heart-shape cutter.

c. Lightly brush the bottom edge with water. Place the flower centre in the middle of the petal, slightly biased to one side. Wrap the petal over, adhering only the bottom edge to the base of the flower centre.

d. Repeat until desired number of calla lilies are formed.

e. Hook calla lilies upside down on a rack. Leave to dry overnight.

10. Straighten flower stems and carefully insert them into the cake.

Blue Fantasy

Equipment

- Serrated knife
- Rolling pin
- Round cutter, about 3 mm ($\frac{1}{8}$ in) wider than the cupcakes
- Fleur de lis cake stencil
- Angled spatula
- Daisy cutters of various sizes
- Flower setter or painter's palette
- Ruler
- Blade tool
- Any cylindrical shaped tool, about 3.5 cm ($1\frac{1}{2}$ in) in diameter
- Paintbrush or airbrush
- Square cutters, 1 slightly smaller than the other

Ingredients

- Cupcakes
- Buttercream
- Fondant — white, teal-blue
- Royal icing
- Water for brushing
- Flower paste — white, light grey
- Icing (confectioner's) sugar or corn flour (cornstarch) for dusting
- Edible silver beads
- Edible lustre dust — silver
- Clear liquor or water for painting

Numbers correspond to the steps on pages 46–49.

4. Fleur de Lis Cupcake 5. Diamond Ring Cupcake
6. Jewelled Cupcake 7. Fancy Bow Cupcake

METHOD

1. Prepare cupcakes for decoration. Trim cupcake tops to get a flat surface, then coat the tops with buttercream to help the fondant adhere to the cupcakes.

2. Prepare icing for cupcake tops. Roll out white and teal-blue fondant until about 3 mm ($1/_8$ in) thick. For teal-blue icing, tint teal, turquoise or sky-blue fondant with a tinge of lime green colouring before rolling it out.

3. Using a round cutter, about 3 mm ($1/_8$ in) wider than the cupcakes, cut out rounds of fondant. Gently attach fondant rounds to cupcake tops. For Fleur de Lis Cupcakes, complete Steps 4a–c before attaching fondant rounds to the cupcakes.

4. Assemble Fleur de Lis Cupcake.

4b

4c

4d

4f

a. Mix about 1 tsp royal icing with water in a bowl, adjusting the amounts until a smooth and soft consistency is achieved. Note that it should not be runny.

b. Place a fleur de lis stencil onto rolled out blue fondant. Using an angled spatula, spread royal icing over the stencil. Move spatula from one side to the other, applying equal force throughout to scrape away any excess.

c. Carefully lift stencil. The patterns should be traced out nicely onto the fondant.

d. Using the same round cutter for the fondant top, press onto patterned fondant. Attach fondant round onto coated cupcake top.

e. For the daisy, roll out white flower paste until about 2 mm ($^1/_8$ in) thick for daisies. Dust a daisy cutter with icing sugar or corn flour, then press onto flower paste to cut out daisies.

f. Carefully lift daisies and place into a flower setter or painter's palette. Leave to dry overnight. Secure silver beads to the centre of each daisy with royal icing.

g. Secure daisies onto cupcake with a dab of royal icing.

5. Assemble Diamond Ring Cupcake.

5b

a. For the ring, tint a small ball of white flower paste with a tiny drop of black colouring to achieve a light grey colour. Roll out flower paste thinly. Using a ruler and a blade tool, cut out a strip for the ring.

b. Lightly dust surface of cylindrical tool with icing sugar or corn flour. Wrap the flower paste strip over the surface of the cylinder, allowing the ends to overlap a bit. Seal the joint and trim away excess. Leave the ring to dry overnight.

c. Mix some silver lustre dust with a bit of clear liquor or water. Using a paintbrush, apply a thin layer of lustre to the ring inside out. Leave to dry for about 30 minutes before applying the next layer. You may use an airbrush to achieve a more even coat of colour.

d. For the daisy settings, form 1 bigger daisy and 2 smaller ones by following the steps for daisies in Fleur de Lis Cupcake.

e. Attach the biggest daisy to the joint on the ring. Place the 2 smaller daisies on either side of the biggest flower.

f. Dab royal icing in the middle of a cupcake. Lightly press to secure diamond ring onto cupcake. Hold the ring upright for a while. Once royal icing starts to crust, the ring is secure.

6. Assemble Jewelled Cupcake.

a. Roll out some blue fondant until about 2 mm ($^1/_8$ in) thick.

b. Using the larger square cutter, press onto fondant to cut out a square piece. Press the smaller square cutter into the middle of the square piece to cut out a hole. You should get a square frame.

c. On the rolled out blue fondant, cut out strips, each the same width as the square frame.

d. Arrange strips and frame over cupcake, securing them to the cupcake with a light brush of water. Trim away excess.

e. Fix silver beads along the insides of the frame with some royal icing.

7. Assemble Fancy Bow Cupcake.

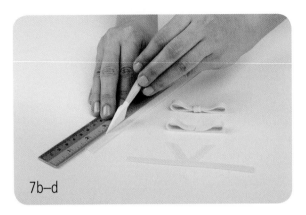

7b–d

a. Roll out some blue fondant.

b. Cut out strips like the ones for Jewelled Cupcake.

c. Assemble the bow. Place a long strip on a flat surface. This is the base for the bow. Join two shorter strips to the middle of the base to form the tails. Trim the ends of the tails such that they are angled.

d. Cut out another long strip. Bring both of its ends towards its middle to form two loops. Join the two loops, hiding the joint with a strip of fondant. Secure with a little water.

e. Attach joined loops on top of the base of the bow with a light brush of water.

f. To give the bow more height, stuff the loops with some tissue until fondant has set.

g. Remove tissue and secure bow to the cupcake with light brushes of water.

h. Fix silver beads all around with royal icing.

Pure Bliss

Equipment

- Serrated knife
- Rolling pin
- Round cutters of various sizes
- Daisy cutters of various sizes
- Flower setter or painter's palette
- Ruler
- Blade tool
- Separate paintbrushes for dry and wet applications
- Foam pad
- Bone tool
- Moulds of various patterns
- Hydrangea- or four-petal flower cutter
- Small round piping tip and piping bag
- Patterned stencil

Ingredients

- Cupcakes
- Buttercream
- Fondant — white
- Icing (confectioner's) sugar or corn flour (cornstarch) for dusting
- Royal icing
- Edible ivory beads
- Water for brushing
- Edible pearl dust

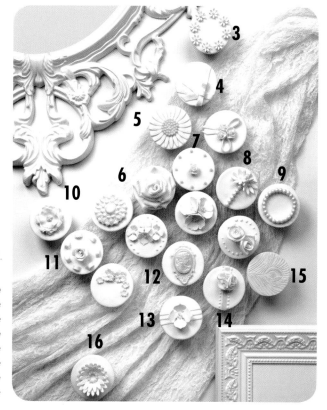

Numbers correspond to the steps on pages 52–57.

3. Ring of Daisies Cupcake   4. Sweet Ribbon Cupcake
5. Gerber (African Daisy) Cupcake   6. Rose Cupcake
7. Pearly Rose Cupcake   8. Pearl and Daisies Cupcake
9. Pearly Cupcake   10. Ruffled Petals Cupcake
11. Rose Corsage Cupcake   12. Fairy Cameo Cupcake
13. Hydrangea Cupcake   14. Frilly Ruffles Cupcake
15. Regal Peacock Feather Cupcake
16. Dual-layered Daisy Cupcake

METHOD

1. Prepare cupcakes for decoration. Trim cupcake tops to get a flat surface, then coat the tops with buttercream to help the fondant adhere to the cupcakes.

2. Prepare icing for cupcake tops. Roll out fondant until about 3 mm ($^1/_8$ in) thick. Using a round cutter, about 3 mm ($^1/_8$ in) wider than the cupcakes, cut out rounds of fondant. Gently attach fondant rounds onto cupcakes.

3. Assemble Ring of Daisies Cupcake.

   a. Roll out fondant until about 2 mm ($^1/_8$ in) thick.

   b. Dust a small daisy cutter with icing sugar or corn flour and press onto fondant to cut out 8 small daisies. Carefully place daisies into a flower setter or painter's palette. Leave overnight to set.

   c. Using a tiny amount of royal icing, fix an ivory bead into each daisy as the flower centre.

   d. Use royal icing to attach daisies along the circumference of the cupcake.

4. Assemble Sweet Ribbon Cupcake.

   a. Roll out fondant. Using a ruler and a blade tool, cut several strips, each about 6 mm ($^1/_4$ in) wide.

   b. Using light brushes of water, attach 2 fondant strips onto cupcake such that they form an off-centre cross. Trim away excess fondant.

   c. Assemble the bow. On a flat surface, bring two ends of a fondant strip towards the centre to form two loops. If you wish to have a fuller bow, stuff some tissue into the loop before sealing the loop ends with some water. Leave tissue in the loops as the fondant sets overnight, removing only when fondant has dried.

   d. Meanwhile, assemble ribbon tails. Bring two short fondant strips to the ribbon base on the cupcake. Each tail should be angled out at 45 degrees. Trim away excess and attach tails to cupcake with light brushes of water.

   e. Once fondant loops have set, wrap a fondant strip around the centre to hide the joint, securing with a little water. Attach onto ribbon base with a light brush of water.

5. Assemble Gerber (African Daisy) Cupcake.

   a. Roll out fondant until about 2 mm ($^1/_8$ in) thick.

   b. Pick a daisy cutter that is the same size as a cupcake top. Dust with icing sugar or corn flour, then press onto fondant to cut out a daisy.

   c. Lightly brush the underside of the daisy with water, then attach on top of cupcake. Use ivory beads to form the flower centre, securing the beads with royal icing.

6. Assemble Rose Cupcake.

6c

6d

6e

6g

   a. Roll out fondant thinly. Using round cutters, cut out fondant rounds for the petals. Use bigger cutters to make larger petals further away from the rose centre. Reserve fondant rounds of different sizes for base petals.

   b. On a foam pad, thin out the edges of fondant rounds with a bone tool to form petals.

   c. Assemble the rose. Shape the core by rolling fondant into a teardrop shape. Wrap each petal over the core, using larger petals for layers that are further out.

d. Shape petals such that they curl out at the edges, as the petals of a rose would. Continue to add and shape petals until rose is complete.

e. Meanwhile, assemble base petals. On a foam pad, use a bone tool to thin out the edges until each piece resembles a rose petal. Arrange petals over cupcake such that it drapes slightly over the cupcake top. Gently fluff the edges of petals.

f. For the second base layer, make slightly smaller petals. Arrange the second layer over the first such that each petal overlaps the intersection of petals on the first layer. Brush lightly with a bit of water to secure petals.

g. For the third base layer, make smaller petals than the second layer. Attach onto the second layer in the same manner, then fix the rose at the centre with some royal icing.

7. Assemble Pearly Rose Cupcake.

a. Assemble a ribbon rose. See Steps 6a–c on page 84.

b. Pipe small pearls of royal icing onto cupcake in a circle. Using royal icing, fix the ribbon rose in the centre.

8. Assemble Pearl and Daisies Cupcake.

a. Form two daisies. See Step 3.

b. Form a chain of pearls. See Step 9.

c. Using royal icing, attach daisies next to pearls onto cupcake.

9. Assemble Pearly Cupcake.

9a–b

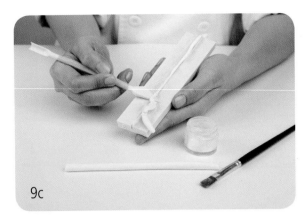

a. Dust a pearl mould with pearl dust. This gives the fondant pearls a shimmer, and also aids with removal from the mould.

b. Using both hands, roll out a ball of fondant, moving both palms in opposite directions, until a long tube is formed. Fit into the pearl mould, then close and squeeze.

c. Trim away excess fondant with a blade tool.

d. Open the mould to release fondant pearls. Attach chain of pearls onto cupcake with light brushes of water.

10. Assemble Ruffled Petals Cupcake.

a. Roll out fondant thinly. Using round cutters of different sizes, press onto fondant to cut out several round pieces.

b. On a foam pad, thin out the edges of fondant rounds with a bone tool to create ruffled petals. Stack ruffled petals on top of one another, with the bigger ones below. Attach ivory beads to the centre using a little royal icing.

c. Attach ruffled petals onto cupcake with royal icing.

11. Assemble Rose Corsage Cupcake.

a. Assemble a rose like in Steps 6a–d, but smaller.

b. Roll out fondant. Using a ruler, cut out a 6 mm ($^1/_4$ in) wide strip. Divide into 7 equal strips, each 2.5 cm (1 in) long. Shape each strip into a semi-circle and arrange them in a circle on the cupcake, attaching them to the cupcake with light brushes of water. Using royal icing, fix the rose in the centre.

12. Assemble Fairy Cameo Cupcake.

a. Dust cameo mould with pearl dust. Roll a ball of fondant about the size of the mould. Press fondant into the cavity and trim away excess.

b. Unmould and attach onto cupcake with a little water.

13. Assemble Hydrangea Cupcake.

a. Form a hydrangea. Roll out fondant thinly and press a hydrangea- or four-petal flower cutter onto it.

b. Carefully place into a flower setter or painter's palette. Leave overnight to set.

c. When hydrangea has set, attach four ivory beads to the flower centre with royal icing.

d. Roll out fondant. Using a ruler as a guide. Cut three strips, each about 3 mm ($^1/_8$ in) wide. Attach onto centre of cupcake with light brushes of water.

e. Attach hydrangea onto strips with a little royal icing.

14. Assemble Frilly Ruffles Cupcake.

a. Roll out fondant thinly. Using a ruler, cut out a 1.5 cm ($^3/_4$ in) wide strip. Attach across cupcake with a light brush of water. Trim away excess.

b. Using a small round piping tip, pipe small dots of royal icing along both sides of fondant strip.

c. Assemble ruffles. Roll out fondant thinly. Press a 4-cm ($1^3/_4$-in) round cutter onto fondant to cut out several round pieces.

d. Hold the edge of one round piece with four fingers — the middle finger and thumb of each hand. Leave index fingers free to move. Press inwards with index fingers to create a ruffle. Repeat to make five ruffles.

e. Gather the ruffles to make a half ball. Attach onto cupcake, over the fondant strip, with a little royal icing.

15. Assemble Regal Peacock Feather Cupcake. See Steps 4a–d on pages 46–47, but use a stencil with peacock feather patterns.

16. Assemble Dual-layered Daisy Cupcake.

a. Roll out fondant until about 2 mm ($^1/_8$ in) thick.

b. Pick two daisy cutters of different sizes. Dust with icing sugar or corn flour and press onto fondant to cut out daisies. Carefully place daisies into a flower setter or painter's palette. Leave overnight to set.

c. Attach the smaller daisy on top of the bigger one with a little royal icing. Using small dabs of royal icing, fix ivory beads to make the flower centre. Attach onto cupcake with royal icing.

17. For the rest of the cupcakes, follow the basic steps outlined above and use patterned moulds and cutters of your choice.

Be My Valentine

Equipment

- Black satin ribbon
- Craft glue or hot glue
- Rolling pin
- Ruler
- Blade tool
- Paintbrush
- Round cutter

Ingredients

- Single-tiered square cake
- Fondant — soft pink, black, white
- Water for brushing
- Edible dust — charcoal
- Clear liquor or water for painting

METHOD

1. Prepare for decoration, following instructions in Sections A–D on pages 26–31.

   a. Use soft pink fondant to cover the cake.

   b. Decorate cake board by adhering black satin ribbon to the side with glue.

2. For the black ribbon on the cake, roll out black fondant until about 2 mm ($^1/_8$ in) thick. Using a ruler and a blade tool, trim fondant into a 0.5 x 40-cm ($^1/_4$ x 16-in) strip. Apply light brushes of water to one side of the strip, then attach it across the centre of the cake. Trim away excess.

3. For the pink border at the bottom edges, roll out soft pink fondant until about 2 mm ($^1/_8$ in) thick. Using a ruler and a blade tool, trim fondant into a 2 x 40-cm (1 x 16-in) strip. Apply light brushes of water to one side of the strip. Adhere pink border to the bottom edges of half of the cake first without covering the black ribbon. Trim away excess. Repeat for the other half of the cake to complete the pink border.

4. Assemble white ruffles.

4d

a. Roll out fondant thinly. Press a round cutter onto fondant to cut out round pieces.

b. Hold the edge of one round piece with four fingers — the middle finger and thumb of each hand. Leave index fingers free to move. Press inwards with index fingers to create a ruffle. Repeat to make enough ruffles for decorating cake. (See page 56.)

c. Trim the bottom end of each ruffle.

d. Arrange trimmed flat ends of ruffles to sit nicely along both sides of the black ribbon. Attach ruffles to the cake with light brushes of water.

5. Assemble black ribbon bow.

5b–c

a. Roll out black fondant until about 2 mm (¹/₈ in) thick. Using a ruler and a blade tool, trim fondant into three strips, one 0.5 x 5 cm (¹/₄ x 2 in), the next 0.5 x 8 cm (¹/₄ x 3 in), and the last 0.5 x 10 cm (¹/₄ x 4 in).

b. Bring the longest strip into a V shape, with both ends of equal length. Gently pinch the V-tip until the strip resembles ribbon tails.

c. Bring both ends of the medium-length strip to the centre to form two ribbon loops. Use a light brush of water to hold the ends in position. Place the shortest strip centrally behind the ribbon loops. Gently fold over to conceal the loops joints. Trim away excess.

6. Attach ribbon tails and loops to the cake with light brushes of water.

7. Mix charcoal dust with clear liquor or water. Using a fine brush, paint text as desired onto the cake.

Adorable Zodiac Dozen

Equipment

- Serrated knife
- Rolling pin
- Round cutters of various sizes
- Separate paintbrushes for dry and wet applications

Ingredients

- Cupcakes
- Buttercream
- Fondant — various colours
- Edible dusts — charcoal, pink, light red
- Clear liquor or water for painting

METHOD

1. Prepare cupcakes for decoration. Trim cupcake tops to get a flat surface, then coat the tops with buttercream to help the fondant adhere to the cupcakes.

2. Prepare icing for cupcake tops. Roll out fondant until about 3 mm ($^1/_8$ in) thick. For each icing top, tint fondant with colour before rolling it out. The colours used here are off white, pastel pink, pastel blue and peach pink. To get peach pink, tint pink fondant with a tinge of orange. You can use other colours if you prefer.

3. Using a round cutter, about 3 mm ($^1/_8$ in) wider than the cupcakes, cut out rounds of fondant. Gently attach fondant rounds to cupcake tops.

4. Assemble the sheep.

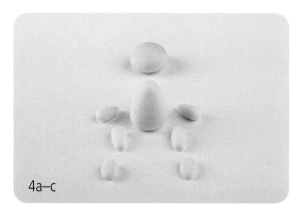
4a–c

4d–e

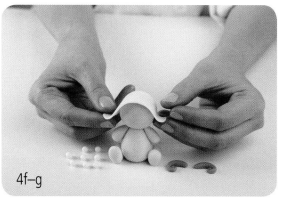
4f–g

4g

4h–i

a. Roll pink fondant into a ball. Shape into an oval for the body.

b. Roll ivory fondant into a ball. This will be the head.

c. Roll pink fondant into four small balls, then shape each ball into a cylindrical shape, with one end slightly tapered, for the limbs.

d. Attach limbs to the body with light brushes of water.

e. Insert a toothpick into the body, leaving a third of the toothpick exposed. Attach the head to form the complete body.

f. Roll out pink fondant thinly. Press a small round cutter onto fondant to cut out a round piece. Drape over the head as a headdress.

g. Shape white fondant into several small balls, and brown fondant into two curled horns. Attach to the headdress with light brushes of water.

h. Attach a tiny ivory fondant ball as the nose.

i. Use charcoal dust for the eyes and red for the mouth. Mix each colour with clear liquor or water. Using a fine brush, paint the face as desired. To add blushes, apply light pink dust to the cheeks with a dry brush.

j. Attach sheep to the cupcake with royal icing.

5. Assemble the rest of the animals by following the steps for the sheep, but use different colours as desired.

6. For the animal ears, roll two small fondant balls. Press lightly to flatten into discs. Press a tiny fondant ball of another colour into the centre of each disc. Shape the ears accordingly for each animal. Flatten one portion of each ear and attach to the headdress with light brushes of water.

7. For the dragon's headdress, assemble fondant pieces as shown. Attach each piece to the headdress with light brushes of water.

8. For the snake's headdress, roll a ball of green fondant into a tube with a tapered end. Coil the tube, with the tapered end at the bottom. Pinch the top so that it resembles a snake's head. Attach to the headdress with a light brush of water.

9. For the black patterns on the cow, tiger and rooster, roll some black fondant and shape the patterns accordingly before adhering to the animals with a little water.

Golden Longevity Cake

Equipment

- Gold ribbon
- Craft glue or hot glue
- Rolling pin
- Cone tool
- Separate paintbrushes for dry and wet applications
- Rotary cutter
- Round cutter
- Leaf-shaper tool

Ingredients

- Two round cake tiers of different sizes
- Fondant — peach, gold
- Flower paste — gold
- Royal icing
- Edible lustre dusts — gold, pink
- Water for brushing
- Clear liquor or water for painting

METHOD

1. Prepare for decoration, following instructions in Sections A–D on pages 26–31.

   a. Use peach fondant to cover each tier. To get peach fondant, mix pink fondant with a tinge of orange.

   b. Decorate cake board by adhering gold ribbon to the side with glue.

2. Assemble cake tiers. See instructions in Section E on pages 32–33.

3. Assemble peaches.

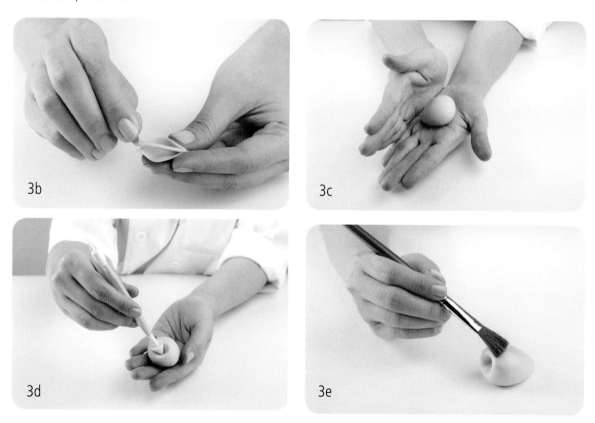

   a. Roll a small round of gold flower paste into a ball, then apply pressure using both palms, moving in opposite directions, to roll flower paste into a small stem. Repeat to make another stem.

   b. Roll out gold flower paste thinly. Using a rotary cutter, cut out two leaves. Lightly fold each leaf into half lengthwise and attach to each stem with a tiny bit of royal icing. Leave to dry overnight.

3g

c. Shape peach fondant into a ball. Moving both palms in opposite directions, shape until it is tapered on one end, like an inverted water droplet. Repeat to shape another peach.

d. Using a cone tool, gently dent the centre of each rounded end.

e. To add a natural pink glow to the peaches, use a dry paintbrush to apply pink lustre dust onto desired areas on the peaches.

f. Apply a tiny bit of water into the dent. Attach stem and leaf at the dent. Repeat for the other peach.

g. Mix gold lustre dust with some liquor or water. Paint the stems and leaves to give them a gold shimmer.

4. Assemble longevity tree.

4b

a. Roll a gold round of fondant into a ball, then shape into a lengthy rope tapered at one end. Attach to the cake from the bottom tier all the way to the top with light brushes of water. Gently shape the fondant such that it snakes out like a branch. Press trunk and branches with fingers to create dents like the uneven surface of a tree.

b. Create fans. Roll out fondant until about 2 mm ($^1/_8$ in) thick. Using a round cutter, cut out round fondant pieces. Halve each round with a rotary cutter. Using a leaf-shaper tool, make lines on each half so that they resemble fans. Attach fans to the branches with light brushes of water.

c. Mix gold lustre dust with some liquor or water. Paint the tree to give it a gold shimmer.

5. Top cake with peaches.

Equipment

- Pink ribbon
- Craft glue or hot glue
- Rolling pin
- Measuring tape
- Ruler
- Cutter or small knife
- Separate paintbrushes for dry and wet applications
- Round cutters of various sizes
- Butterfly cutters of various sizes
- Small cardboard pieces
- Ball tool
- Foam pad
- Craft scissors (optional)
- Tissue (optional)
- Toothpicks

Ingredients

- Single-tiered round cake
- Fondant — Sky blue, white, baby pink, ivory, black
- Water for brushing
- Flower paste — baby pink
- Icing (confectioner's) sugar or corn flour (cornstarch)
- Edible dusts — charcoal, brown, pink
- Clear liquor or water for painting
- Royal icing

METHOD

1. Prepare for decoration, following instructions in Sections A–D on pages 26–31.

   a. Use sky blue fondant to cover the cake.

   b. Decorate cake board by adhering pink ribbon to the side with glue.

2. For the white border at the bottom of the cake, use a measuring tape or ribbon to measure the circumference of the cake first. Roll out fondant until about 2 mm ($\frac{1}{8}$ in) thick, and to the length of the cake's circumference. Trim fondant into a straight ribbon. Apply light brushes of water to one side, then adhere to the bottom of the cake.

3. For the pink squares on the border, roll out pink fondant until about 2 mm ($\frac{1}{8}$ in) thick, and slightly shorter than the length of the cake's circumference. Trim into squares of the same height as the white border. Adhere to the white border with light brushes of water.

4. For the polka dots, roll out white fondant until about 2 mm ($\frac{1}{8}$ in) thick. Using a round cutter, cut out small round polka dots and adhere to the cake with light brushes of water.

5. Form butterflies.

5a–b

   a. Roll out baby pink flower paste thinly. Dust butterfly cutters with icing sugar or corn flour and press onto flower paste to cut out butterflies of various sizes.

   b. Fold cardboard pieces in half so that it resembles an L or V shape when released. Leave butterflies to set at the crease of the cardboards.

6. Form ballerina legs.

6d

a. Roll ivory fondant into a ball. Place the ball in the centre of a palm, then roll with both palms in opposite directions until it lengthens into a cylindrical tube tapered at one end. Shape tapered end into a ballerina's foot. Repeat to form another leg.

b. Form ballerina shoes. Roll a small ball of baby pink fondant. Create a small dent in the centre with a ball tool. Apply a little water to the dent and fit it over a foot. Shape to resemble a ballet shoe. Repeat for the other leg.

c. Roll out baby pink fondant thinly. Using a ruler, cut into four long thin strips, each double the length of a leg.

d. Lightly brush one side of a strip with water. Wind the strip around a leg, starting from the shoe. Lightly brush another strip with water and wind around the leg such that it criss-crosses the other strip. Repeat for the other leg.

7. Form the tutu.

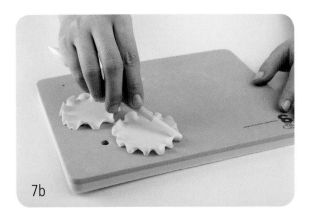

7b

a. Roll out baby pink fondant until about 2 mm ($^1/_8$ in) thick. Press a round cutter onto the fondant to cut out a few round pieces.

b. On a foam pad, press a ball tool onto each fondant round to dent and thin out the edge. Each ruffle should be about 0.5 mm ($^1/_4$ in) apart.

8. Form the torso.

a. Roll ivory fondant into a ball, then shape into a rectangle for the torso. Gently dent the top corners so that they slope like shoulders. Shape the lower end such that it is slightly tapered to form the ballerina's waist.

b. For the leotard, roll out baby pink fondant thinly, then trim into a rectangular piece. Lightly brush leotard with water before wrapping around the torso. Trim away excess. Attach two thin strips over the shoulders to complete the leotard.

9. Form the arms.

a. Pinch a small amount of ivory fondant. Shape into a ball and place it in the middle of a palm. Use a finger of the other hand to shape the arm, moving palm and finger in opposite directions, until one end is slightly tapered. Repeat to form the other arm.

b. Slightly flatten the tapered end of one arm. Snip a small v so that it resembles a hand. Use craft scissors to shape the fingers if desired. Repeat for the other arm.

10. Form the head.

a. Roll some ivory fondant into a ball.

b. Attach tiny ivory fondant beads as nose and ears.

c. Roll out black fondant thinly. Drape over the head and shape hairstyle as desired.

11. Assemble the ballerina.

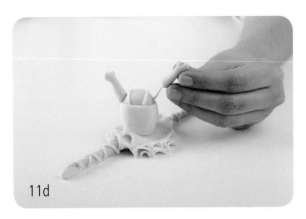

11d

   a. Using a light brush of water, join the two legs such that the ballerina is in a split position. Lightly brush the portion where the tutu will be attached with a little water.

   b. Attach tutu on top of ballerina's legs, using light brushes of water to join the centre of each layer to one another. Gently fluff the ruffled layers. To get a fuller tutu, insert a small piece of folded tissue all around between each layer. Remove tissue after fondant sets.

   c. Insert a toothpick into the centre of the torso, leaving one end of the toothpick exposed. Join the torso to the tutu by inserting the exposed part of the toothpick into the centre of the tutu.

   d. Insert two toothpicks into the slopes of the shoulders, leaving the ends exposed to attach the arms.

   e. Insert a toothpick between the shoulders, leaving the end exposed to attach the head.

12. Paint the ballerina's face. Mix edible dusts with clear liquor or water. Use charcoal for the eyes, and brown for the eyebrows and mouth. For the blushes on the cheeks, apply pink dust directly onto the face without mixing with liquor or water.

13. Apply royal icing beneath the legs and attach ballerina to the cake. Finish by attaching butterflies to the cake with a little royal icing.

Happy Wedding Couple

Equipment

- Pink ribbon
- Craft glue or hot glue
- Measuring tape
- Rolling pin
- Decorative template
- Rotary cutter with serrated edges
- Separate paintbrushes for dry and wet applications
- Cookie cutters — round, heart-shaped of various sizes
- Bamboo skewers and toothpicks
- Styrofoam pad
- Ball tool
- Blade tool
- Foam pad

Ingredients

- Single-tiered round cake
- Fondant — pink, peach, white, ivory, black
- Water for brushing
- Royal icing
- Edible dusts — charcoal, brown, pink
- Clear liquor or water for painting

METHOD

1. Prepare for decoration, following instructions in Sections A–D on pages 26–31.

   a. Use pink fondant to cover the cake.

   b. Decorate cake board by adhering pink ribbon to the side with glue.

2. Assemble the cake border.

   a. Measure the circumference of the cake with a measuring tape or ribbon. Roll out peach fondant until about 2 mm ($^1/_8$ in) thick, and to the length of the cake's circumference. Press a decorative template onto the fondant to cut out a patterned border.

   b. Roll out white fondant until about 2 mm ($^1/_8$ in) thick, and to the same length as the peach border. Using a rotary cutter with serrated edges, cut a strip of wavy ribbon.

c. Apply light brushes of water to one side of white ribbon, then adhere
      to the bottom of the peach border.

   d. Apply light brushes of water to the underside of the peach border
      and attach to the bottom of the cake.

3. Assemble the dais.

   a. Roll peach fondant into a ball, then flatten until it is a disc about
      1 cm ($^1/_2$ in) thick.

   b. Press a round cutter onto fondant to cut out a round dais for the
      couple to stand on.

   c. Line the side of the dais with white fondant strip, like the one for the
      peach border in Step 2b.

   d. Attach to the cake with royal icing.

4. Assemble the groom.

4a

4c

4e

4f

4g

4h–i

a. Form the legs. Roll white fondant into a ball. Push a skewer through the centre until it is at the middle of the skewer. Shape the ball into a cylinder, leaving the bottom half and 0.5 mm ($^1/_4$ in) at the top exposed. Push the bottom half of the skewer into a Styrofoam pad. Repeat to make the other leg. Join both legs side-by-side with a light brush of water.

b. Form the shoes. Roll white fondant into a small ball. Using a ball tool, create a dent to fit the leg as a shoe. Attach to the leg with a light brush of water. Repeat for the other leg.

c. Insert a skewer where the legs join. Leave a sufficient part of the skewer exposed for attaching the torso and head.

d. Form the torso. Roll white fondant into a ball. Shape into a rectangle. Round the top edges to resemble shoulders. Centrally align torso to the legs and attach by pushing into the exposed part of the skewer.

e. Make the groom's suit. Roll out a rectangular piece of white fondant until about 2 mm ($^1/_8$ in) thick. Hold it around the torso to measure out the size of the suit. Trim away excess.

f. Cut a V at the back of the suit, then trim the front to resemble a buttoned suit.

g. Attach the suit to the torso with light brushes of water.

h. Form the arms. Roll white fondant into a small ball, then shape into a cylindrical tube. Trim one end to flatten, then, using a ball tool, create a dent where the hand will fit. Repeat to make the other arm.

i. Roll a small bit of ivory fondant into a ball. Flatten into a disc and shape into a hand and wrist. Use a blade tool to carve out the fingers. Attach hand to the dent in the arm with a little water. Repeat for the other hand.

j. Insert a toothpick on each side of the groom to attach arms. Further secure arms to the torso with light brushes of water.

k. Form the head. Roll ivory fondant into a ball. Roll out black fondant thinly. Drape over the head and shape hairstyle as desired.

5. Assemble the bride.

5b

5c

5d

a. Roll ivory fondant into a ball, then shape into a cylinder with both palms moving in opposite directions. To shape the waist, exert more force at the part about one-third from the top until an hourglass shape is achieved.

b. Make the bridal gown. Roll out white fondant until about 2 mm ($^1/_8$ in) thick. Hold it around the bride to measure out the size of the gown. Trim away excess until it is a tube gown and attach it to the bride with light brushes of water.

c. Form the arms. Roll ivory fondant into a ball, then shape into two cylinders. Attach to the bride with light brushes of water. Gently shape arms until they curve towards the front.

d. Form bride's hair. Roll out black fondant thinly. Drape over the head and lightly carve hair strands with a blade tool. For the braid, roll black fondant into a thin tube and taper both ends. Bring both ends together and twist into a braid, starting from the bend of the loop. Attach braid to the bride with a light brush of water.

6. Assemble bouquet of roses.

6c

a. Roll out peach fondant thinly. Use a blade tool to cut fondant into several strips.

b. On a foam pad, thin out the top edge with a ball tool.

c. Apply a light brush of water to the bottom edge. Pinch one lower edge inwards and roll up the strip, gathering the bottom into a tight bunch while leaving the top loose to resemble rose petals. Taper the bottom so that it is easier to gather all the roses in a bunch later on. Repeat until there are enough roses to form the bouquet.

d. Gather the roses into a bouquet and attach to the bride with royal icing.

e. Form a larger rose for the bride's headpiece. Attach to the bride's hair with royal icing.

7. Paint the faces of the couple. Mix edible dusts with clear liquor or water. Use charcoal for the eyes, and brown for the eyebrows, nose and mouth. For the blushes on the cheek, use a dry paintbrush to apply pink dust for a healthy glow.

8. Attach couple onto the dais with royal icing.

9. Form heart-shape patterns. Roll out white fondant until about 2 mm ($^1/_8$ in) thick. Press heart-shape cutters onto fondant to cut out heart-shape pieces. Attach to cake with light brushes of water.

Sparkling White Christmas

Equipment

- Red ribbon
- Craft glue or hot glue
- Rolling pin
- Cone former, or stiff paper shaped into a cone
- Blade tool
- Rotary cutter
- Foam pad
- Leaf tool
- Paintbrush
- Tissue
- Various cutters — snowflakes of various sizes, holly leaf

Ingredients

- Single-tiered round cake
- Flower paste — white
- Fondant — white, red
- Corn flour (cornstarch)
- Water for brushing
- Edible lustre dust — silver
- Clear liquor or water for painting
- Royal icing

METHOD

1. Prepare for decoration, following instructions in Sections A–D on pages 26–31.

   a. Decorate cake board by adhering red ribbon to the side with royal icing.

2. Assemble Christmas tree.

2a

2e

2f

2g

2h

a. Roll out flower paste thinly, then wrap around a cone former. Using a blade tool, trace the shape of the cone. Remove from cone former and trim accordingly, leaving some allowance.

b. Wrap trimmed flower paste around the cone former, but not too tightly, so that it can be easily removed when dry. Leave to stand overnight until it sets. Remove cone former to dry the inside of the flower paste cone. Leave overnight to dry completely.

c. Form the leaves. Knead some white fondant. Mix in corn flour to get a dryer texture, but not too dry until it cracks. Roll out fondant mixture until about 3 mm ($^1/_8$ in) thick.

d. Using a rotary cutter, cut several 3.5 cm ($1^1/_2$ in) strips.

e. Using a blade tool, cut out alternating triangles from each strip.

f. On a foam pad, use a leaf tool to shape each triangle into a leaf. Press two to three times, starting near the tip to the base of the triangle, until the tip curls up like a leaf. Turn over and lightly brush the straight edge with water.

g. Attach to the bottom of the flower paste cone and let the leaves fan out.

h. Shape and attach leaves layer by layer until the entire tree is covered. Insert rolls of tissue all around between each layer of leaves.

i. Leave Christmas tree to dry and set overnight. Remove tissue only when fondant has set so that the curves do not collapse.

3. Roll out flower paste until about 2 mm ($^{1}/_{8}$ in) thick. Press snowflake cutters onto flower paste to cut out snowflake shapes of various sizes. Leave to set and dry overnight.

4. Assemble holly plant.

a. Roll out flower paste until about 2 mm ($^{1}/_{8}$ in) thick. Press a holly leaf cutter onto flower paste to cut out leaves. Leave to dry overnight.

b. Mix silver lustre dust with liquor or water and paint the leaves. Set aside to dry before painting the next coat.

c. When holly leaves are dry, assemble the plant with red fondant balls as the holly fruits.

d. Make enough holly plants to decorate the cake.

5. Decorate the cake with the Christmas tree, snowflakes and holly plant. Use royal icing to secure the decorations to the cake.

Note: For the leaves of the Christmas tree, use flower paste instead of fondant if desired, so that the shape of the leaves retains better.

Under the Sea

Equipment

- Gold ribbon
- Craft glue or hot glue
- Seashell moulds of various designs and sizes
- Rolling pin
- Rotary cutter
- Bulbous cone tool
- Serrated cone tool
- Blade tool
- Cone tool
- Paintbrush

Ingredients

- Two round cake tiers of different sizes
- Fondant — Royal blue, white, brown, red, purplish-blue, bright orange, pink, yellow
- Icing (confectioner's) sugar or corn flour (cornstarch)
- Flower paste — light green
- Water for brushing
- Edible dust — charcoal
- Clear liquor or water for painting.
- Royal icing

METHOD

1. Prepare for decoration, following instructions in Sections A–D on pages 26–31.

    a. Use royal blue fondant to cover each tier.

    b. Decorate cake board by adhering gold ribbon to the side with glue.

2. Assemble cake tiers. See instructions in Section E on pages 32–33.

3. Form seashells.

3b

    a. Gather a small amount of white fondant. Mix in a little brown fondant. Knead just enough to smooth out lines. Do not over-knead so that a marbling effect is achieved.

    b. Dust seashell moulds with icing sugar or corn flour. Press fondant into seashell moulds. Trim away excess and gently unmould.

4. Form spiral seaweed. Roll out light green flower paste thinly. Using a rotary cutter, slice into pointed strips. Twist each strip several times until a spiral is formed.

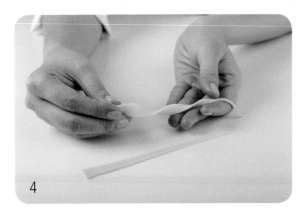

5. Form corals.

a. Roll red fondant into a ball, then shape into an inverted teardrop with both palms moving in opposite directions.

b. Dent the rounded end with a bulbous cone tool.

c. Prepare purplish-blue fondant. To achieve this colour, mix purple fondant with royal blue fondant. Roll into a ball, then form an irregular shape. Press a serrated cone tool onto fondant to create patterns like those on corals. Repeat to make enough corals for the cake.

6. Form clown fishes.

6a–c

6d–f

a. Roll bright orange fondant into a ball. Shape to resemble a clownfish. Use a blade tool to carve the mouth. Repeat to shape another fish.

b. Roll out a small ball of white fondant thinly. Cut out strips of uneven widths. Brush one side of each strip with a little water and wrap around each fish, leaving a space in between stripes.

c. Use a blade tool to impress lines on the tails.

d. Make fish eyes. Shape small white fondant discs. On each disc, press a small bead of blue fondant onto it to form the iris.

e. Mix charcoal dust with liquor or water and draw the pupils.

f. Roll two tiny white fondant beads. Press one on each pupil to create a three-dimensional effect. Attach eyes to fishes with light brushes of water.

g. Mix charcoal dust with liquor or water. On the fish, paint black stripes onto the edges of the white stripes.

7. Assemble octopus.

7a

7c–d

a. Follow the sequence in the picture to shape octopus arms. First, roll pink fondant into a ball, then shape with both palms moving in opposite directions until it tapers on one end. Next, shape the rounded end such that it resembles an elongated teardrop. Repeat to make seven arms. The eighth arm will stem from the head.

b. For the suction cups, roll yellow fondant into small beads. Attach to the thicker end of each arm. Use a cone tool to dent the centre of each bead.

c. Roll a ball of pink fondant for the head. With both palms moving in opposite directions, shape two-thirds of the middle portion into a slim arm, with the end rounded like the other arms of the octopus.

d. Press a yellow fondant bead to the head. Using a cone tool, dent the centre of the bead so that it resembles a mouth.

e. Attach eyes like the clown fish ones to the head.

8. Assemble the cake. Arrange octopus head and arms on the cake before attaching with royal icing. Adhere clown fishes, seaweed, corals and seashells to the cake with royal icing.

Fun Sushi Platter

Equipment

- Rolling pin
- Rotary cutter
- Ruler
- Blade tool
- Paintbrush
- Five-petal flower cutters of various sizes

Ingredients

- Single-tiered square cake
- Fondant — black, pink, green, light brown, white, orange, yellow, light brown, dark brown
- Water for brushing
- Edible dust — white, red, yellow
- Clear liquor or water for painting
- Royal icing

METHOD

1. Prepare for decoration, following instructions in Sections A–D on pages 26–31.

1a

   a. Use black fondant to cover the cake. For the top surface, roll out black fondant until 3 mm ($^1/_8$ in) thick. Gently roll a rotary cutter over the fondant sheet to create creases like those on wood. Measure the top surface of the cake and trim fondant accordingly. Apply to the top of the cake.

   b. For the side panels, roll out black fondant until 3 mm ($^1/_8$ in) thick. Using a blade tool, trim into four panels, each 3 mm ($^1/_8$ in) wider and taller than the sides of the cake. Attach one panel to each side of the cake.

2. Make pickled ginger. Roll out pink fondant as thinly as possible. Use the serrated edge of the rotary cutter to trim into irregular long oval strips. Loosely gather several strips together and lightly press to create a serving of pickled ginger.

3. Make wasabi. Roll green fondant into a ball, then shape into a rounded leaf-like shape. Use a blade tool to impress lines on it to resemble a serving of wasabi.

4. Form chopsticks. Roll light brown fondant into a ball. On a flat surface, roll back and forth with palms until the fondant lengthens. Continue rolling until it tapers to a sharp point at one end. Trim the larger end with a blade tool to create a flat top. Repeat to make another chopstick. Leave to dry overnight.

5. Assemble salmon sushi.

a. Form rice clusters for salmon sushi. Roll white fondant into a ball. Shape to resemble two rectangular rice clusters.

b. Form small oval beads of white fondant to resemble rice grains. Adhere to the sides of sushi rice clusters with a light brush of water.

c. Make salmon slices. Roll out orange fondant until about 3 mm ($^1/_8$ in) thick. Roll out white fondant thinly. Use a rotary cutter to trim curvy uneven strips. Lightly brush one side of each strip with water, then arrange them onto orange fondant, unevenly spaced, to resemble salmon fat. Using a rolling pin, press white strips onto the orange fondant.

d. Trim out two salmon slices with a blade tool. Attach on top of rectangular rice cluster with light brushes of water.

6. Assemble maki rolls.

6a

6e

6g

6h

a. Form the egg. Roll out yellow fondant as thinly as possible. Trim into a long strip. Roll it up like an elliptical swiss roll, then trim into two pieces, each 22 mm ($^4/_5$ in) long, with a squarish cross section. Note that the subsequent ingredients should have the same dimensions, as all of them should be uniform.

b. Form mushrooms with light brown and dark brown fondant. You can get different shades of brown by mixing white and brown fondant until you get the desired shades. Roll out light brown fondant until about 5 mm ($^1/_4$ in) thick, and dark brown fondant until about 3 mm ($^1/_8$ in) thick. Attach them together with a light brush of water, then trim into two pieces of the same size as the egg pieces.

c. Form salmon pieces. Roll out orange fondant until about 1 cm ($^1/_2$ in) thick. Trim into two pieces the same size as the egg pieces.

d. Form crab roll. Roll out white fondant as thinly as possible. Roll it up like a swiss roll. Repeat to make another one, trimming each one to be the same size as the egg pieces.

e. Roll out black fondant thinly for the seaweed. Cut into two rectangular strips, each 22 mm ($^4/_5$ in) wide, and long enough to wrap each set of ingredients. Seal the joint with a little water. Trim away excess.

f. Make rice for maki. Roll out white fondant until about 7 mm ($^1/_3$ in) thick. Cut into two long strips, each 20 mm ($^4/_5$ in) wide, and long enough to wrap around each maki roll (6e). Place a maki roll (6e) onto one of the white strips. Position 6e such that it is aligned on one side, but extends by 2 mm ($^1/_8$ in) on the other side. Wrap the white strip around each maki roll and seal the joint with a little water. Trim away excess. Repeat for the other maki roll. Note that the aligned side will be unseen, as it will be adhered to the cake.

g. Roll out another sheet of black fondant thinly for the outer layer of seaweed. Cut into two rectangular strips, each 22 mm ($^4/_5$ in) wide, and long enough to wrap around maki rolls (6f). When wrapped around each maki roll, this layer of seaweed should be aligned all around with the first layer of seaweed. Seal the joint with a little water. Trim away excess.

h. Paint maki rolls only on one side, where the ingredients extend by about 2 mm ($^1/_8$ in). Separately mix white dust and red dust with liquor or water. Using a fine brush, dab red dots onto crab roll to resemble crab meat, and draw irregular white strips onto salmon to resemble salmon fat.

i. Form small oval beads of white fondant to resemble rice grains. Adhere to the rice cluster on the painted side. This will create a level surface, as the rice cluster will now be aligned to the extended ingredients with the addition of rice grains. Repeat for the other maki roll.

7. Form sakura flowers.

a. Roll out pink fondant until about 2 mm ($^1/_8$ in) thick. Press five-petal flower cutters onto fondant to cut out flowers.

b. Mix yellow dust with liquor or water. Brush onto flower centres. Adhere to the cake with some water.

8. Assemble the cake. Adhere chopsticks and food items onto the cake with royal icing.

Pirate-themed Party

Equipment

- Red satin ribbon
- Craft glue or hot glue
- Serrated knife
- Rolling pin
- Round cutter, about 3mm ($1/_8$ in) wider than the cupcakes
- Templates (see page 155)
- Blade tool
- Ruler
- Separate paintbrushes for dry and wet applications
- Toothpicks

Ingredients

- Single-tiered round cake + cupcakes
- Fondant — various shades of blue, ivory, orange, black, light brown, dark brown, white, dark green, light green, yellow
- Buttercream
- Flower paste — brown, orangey-red, white
- Edible dust — white, brown, charcoal
- Clear liquor or water for painting
- Royal icing
- Water for brushing
- Food colouring — black
- Edible lustre dust — silver, gold

METHOD

1. Prepare for decoration, following instructions in Sections A–D on pages 26–31.

   a. Use sky blue fondant to cover the cake.

   b. Decorate cake board by adhering red satin ribbon to the side with glue.

2. Prepare cupcakes for decoration. Trim cupcake tops to get a flat surface, then coat the tops with buttercream to help the fondant adhere to the cupcakes.

3. Prepare icing for cupcake tops. Roll out sky blue fondant until about 5 mm ($^1/_4$ in) thick. Using a round cutter, cut out rounds of fondant. Gently attach fondant rounds to cupcake tops.

4. Make pirate headpieces.

4b

   a. Print the template for pirate headpieces, one large one for the cake and two small ones for the cupcakes.

   b. Roll out brown flower paste until about 2 mm ($^1/_8$ in) thick. Place each headpiece template onto flower paste sheet and trace out the shapes with a blade tool.

   c. Rest headpieces on a curved surface until they have set.

   d. Mix white dust with clear liquor or water. Paint a thick coat of skulls and crossbones onto the headpieces. Set aside to dry. Attach one small headpiece to a cupcake with royal icing. Keep the other small headpiece for the pirate.

   e. Make feathers for headpieces, one large one for the cake, and one small one for the cupcake. Roll out orangey-red flower paste until about 2 mm ($^1/_8$ in) thick. Place each feather template onto flower paste and trace out the shape with a blade tool. Leave to set before attaching to headpieces.

5. Assemble the pirate.

5a–c

a. Roll ivory fondant into a ball. This is the pirate's head. Roll another small ivory bead as the nose.

b. Roll out orange fondant thinly. Trace out a crescent shape for the beard. Shape another two small balls of fondant as the moustache.

c. Roll out black fondant thinly. Cut out a black strip and a round piece for the eye patch.

d. Attach the different parts to the pirate's head with a light brush of water.

e. Secure headpiece with feather onto the pirate with royal icing.

f. Mix charcoal dust with liquor or water. Paint the eyeball.

g Secure pirate to the cupcake with royal icing.

6. Create treasure map.

6b–c

a. Roll out light brown fondant until about 2 mm ($^1/_8$ in) thick. Trim into a 15 cm (6 in) long rectangular strip.

b. Using a blade tool, cut narrow Vs along the top and bottom edges to resemble a tattered map.

c. Using a dry paintbrush, dab the tattered edges with brown dust so that it looks like an old map.

d. Mix charcoal dust with liquor or water. Ink the treasure map as desired. Leave to dry.

e. Roll both ends of treasure map such that it appears as an open scroll. Attach to cupcake with light brushes of water.

7. Form the hook.

   a. Tint white flower paste and white fondant separately with a small amount of black colouring. Knead to mix each of them well.

   b. Roll light grey flower paste into a stick and shape into a hook. Leave to dry overnight.

   c. Roll light grey fondant into a ball. Shape into an oval for the hook base. Using a blade tool, trim to flatten one end. Attach hook to the rounded end of the hook base.

   d. Mix silver lustre dust with liquor or water. Brush onto hook. Leave to dry before attaching to cupcake with royal icing.

8. Assemble the parrot.

8a–b

   a. Gather sufficient dark green and light green fondant. Roll into balls of different sizes, then shape the individual parts of the parrot. Shape yellow fondant as the beak.

   b. For the crown and tail feathers, use a blade tool to impress lines on the dark green fondant pieces to resemble feathers.

   c. Attach the tail to the cupcake with royal icing. Insert a toothpick through the tail, leaving about two-thirds of it exposed. Attach the body through the toothpick, then join the head on top. If the toothpick is not long enough, insert another one through the body to join the head.

   d. Attach the rest of the parts to the parrot with royal icing.

   e. Roll small white fondant beads as eyes. Attach to the head with royal icing. Mix charcoal dust with liquor or water to paint the eyes.

9. Create treasure chest.

   a. Roll dark brown fondant into a ball. Shape into a treasure chest.

   b. Using a blade tool, impress lines onto it to differentiate the container and the lid.

   c. Roll yellow fondant into two strips. Attach to the lid with light brushes of water.

   d. Attach treasure chest to the cupcake with royal icing.

   e. Roll yellow fondant into little discs that resemble gold coins. Attach to cupcake with a light brush of water.

   f. Mix gold lustre dust with liquor or water. Paint over the coins and yellow strips on the treasure chest.

10. Create waves and sailing boats.

   a. For the waves, roll out royal blue fondant until about 2 mm ($^1/_8$ in) thick. Use a blade tool to cut out a series of waves long enough to wrap around the cake. Brush one side with water, then adhere to the bottom of the cake.

   b. For the sailing boats, roll out light blue fondant until about 2 mm ($^1/_8$ in) thick. Place sailing boat template onto fondant sheet and trace out the shape with a blade tool. Make a few sailing boats. Brush each of them with water on one side, then adhere to the cake.

11. Attach the large headpiece with feather to the cake. Use royal icing to secure.

Pretty Carousel

Equipment

- Gold satin ribbon
- Craft glue or hot glue
- One lollipop stick
- Styrofoam pad
- Paintbrush
- Rolling pin
- Template (see page 155)
- Blade tool
- Silicon moulds of various patterns
- Toothpick (optional)
- Round cutter
- Heart-shape cutters of two sizes
- Piping bag

Ingredients

- Single-tiered round cake
- Fondant — yellow, white, green, various shades of pink
- Water for brushing
- Edible lustre dust — gold
- Clear liquor or water for painting
- Flower paste — white
- Royal icing — white, yellow, green
- Icing (confectioner's) sugar or corn flour (cornstarch) for dusting
- Edible dust — pink

METHOD

1. Prepare for decoration, following instructions in Sections A–D on pages 26–31.

    a. Decorate cake board by adhering gold satin ribbon to the side with glue.

2. Decorate the pole.

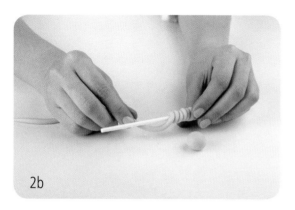

2b

    a. Knead yellow fondant into a ball. Roll with both palms until a lengthy strip of about 3 mm ($^1/_8$ in) thick is formed.

    b. Dampen lollipop stick with water. Beginning at one end, wrap fondant strip around lollipop stick, leaving about 8 cm ($3^1/_8$ in) uncovered. This portion will be inserted into the cake. Roll a small ball of fondant and attach to the top of the pole. Leave to dry upright on a Styrofoam pad.

    c. Mix gold lustre dust with clear liquor or water. Paint the pole and set aside to dry.

3. Assemble the horse.

3b

a. Roll out white flower paste until about 2 mm (¹/₈ in) thick. Place a horse template onto flower paste and trace out the shape with a blade tool. Set aside to dry overnight.

b. Roll small fondant balls into elliptical shapes. Lightly press to flatten each of them. Using a blade tool, impress lines so that they resemble horse hair.

c. Attach horse hair to the horse with royal icing.

d. Mix gold lustre dust with clear liquor or water. Paint the horse hair and set aside to dry.

4. Create flowers and saddle.

4b–c

a. Roll fondant balls of white, green, and various pink shades separately until about 2 mm (¹/₈ in) thick.

b. For the green saddle, dust a silicon heart-shape mould with icing sugar or corn flour. Press green fondant into the mould to form the saddle. Unmould and set aside to dry overnight.

c. For the flowers, dust silicon moulds with icing sugar or corn flour. Press fondant balls into moulds to form various flowers. Unmould and set aside to dry overnight.

d. Pipe a tiny drop of yellow royal icing to flower centres. Set aside to dry overnight.

e. Form daisies. Lightly brush silicon mould with pink dust. Press pink fondant into the mould and trim off excess. Unmould daisies and set aside to dry overnight.

5. Create fancy ropes and frills border.

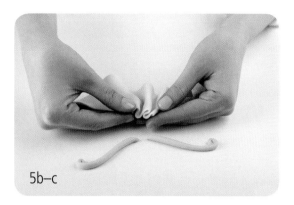

5b–c

a. Using a blade tool or a toothpick, trace the position of the border at the bottom of the cake.

b. Shape fancy ropes. Roll out yellow fondant into a cylindrical strip about 3 mm ($^1/_8$ in) thick. Taper both ends. Shape one end of the rope into a decorative curve. Repeat to make enough fancy ropes to decorate the cake. Attach fancy ropes to the cake according to the traced outline with light brushes of water.

c. Mix gold lustre dust with liquor or water. Paint the fancy ropes and set aside to dry.

d. Shape frills. Roll out pink fondant until about 2 mm ($^1/_8$ in) thick. Press a round cutter to cut out round pieces. Halve each piece. Holding one half, pleat the curved surface. Bunch the pleats at the top. Repeat to make enough frills to decorate cake. Using light brushes of water, attach to the cake, just below the joint of every two fancy ropes.

6. Assemble the carousel.

a. For the carousel platform, gather white fondant to make a platform, or use a fondant-wrapped mini cake.

b. Adhere the horse to the pole with royal icing, leaving about two-thirds uncovered at the bottom. Insert the pole down the centre of the platform.

7. Assemble the cake.

7b

a. Secure the carousel to the cake with royal icing.

b. Roll out green and pink fondant separately for the sugar hearts.
   Press heart-shape cutters onto fondant sheets to cut out the shapes.
   Attach the smaller heart in the centre of the bigger one with a light
   brush of water.

c. Pipe green royal icing as leaves and vines onto cake.

d. Finish by decorating with flowers, attaching them to the cake with
   royal icing.

Road Works

Equipment

- Rolling pin
- Triangle cutter
- Paintbrush
- Blade tool
- Toothpicks
- Square cutter (optional)

Ingredients

- Fondant — white, orange
- Flower paste — red
- Water for brushing
- Edible dust — charcoal
- Clear liquor or water for painting
- Chocolate cupcakes
- Dark chocolate ganache
- Castor sugar, tinted brown
- Royal icing

METHOD

1. Assemble road signs.

1b

a. Roll out white fondant until about 2 mm (¹/₈ in) thick. Press the smaller triangle cutter onto fondant and cut out three pieces. Set aside to dry.

b. Roll out red flower paste until about 2 mm (¹/₈ in) thick, and large enough to fit the three white triangles. Brush one side of each triangle with water and attach to flower paste. Using a blade tool, trim red fondant around white triangles, leaving a border all around.

c. Dampen one end of a toothpick and insert up to 5 mm (¹/₄ in) into the base of each sign. Set aside to dry.

d. Mix charcoal dust with liquor or water. Paint road signs and set aside to dry.

2. Form safety cones.

2b–c

a. Roll orange fondant into a ball. Shape to get a pointed end with both palms moving in opposite directions. Place rounded end on a flat surface and continue to shape into a cone. This way, the rounded end will be flattened as the cone shape forms. Trim the bottom if necessary to get a flatter base. Repeat to make another cone.

b. Roll out orange fondant until 3 mm ($^1/_8$ in) thick. Trim into two square bases for the cones, or use a square cutter. Attach to the cones with light brushes of water.

c. Roll out white fondant thinly. Cut into long strips about 3 mm ($^1/_8$ in) thick each. Lightly brush one side of each strip with water and attach to the cones.

3. Assemble the cupcakes.

3a

a. Pipe chocolate ganache onto cupcakes. Dip into coloured sugar to create a sandy look and texture.

b. Insert road signs onto cupcakes, and attach safety cones to cupcakes with royal icing.

Merry Choo Choo Train

Equipment

- Toothpicks
- Rolling pin
- Ruler
- Blade tool
- Paintbrush
- Star-shape cutters of various sizes
- Several metal stick wires, trimmed accordingly
- Flower cutters of various sizes
- Flower setter or painter's palette
- Round cutters of various sizes

Ingredients

- One square cake, trimmed into four pieces (See Step 1.)
- Fondant — various colours
- Water for brushing
- Flower paste — various colours
- Royal icing — green, yellow
- Edible dust — charcoal
- Clear liquor or water for painting

METHOD

1. Slice cake into the following dimensions:

    a. Rectangular block: 6 cm ($2^1/_2$ in) wide, 12 cm (5 in) long, 6 cm ($2^1/_2$ in) thick, cover with yellow fondant

    b. Rectangular block: 6 cm ($2^1/_2$ in) wide, 6 cm ($2^1/_2$ in) long, 8 cm ($3^1/_8$ in) thick, cover with blue fondant

    c. Rectangular block: 6 cm ($2^1/_2$ in) wide, 3 cm ($1^1/_8$ in) long, 8 cm ($3^1/_8$ in) thick, cover with green fondant

    d. Cylindrical block: 4 cm ($1^3/_4$ in) in diameter, 7.5 cm long (3 in), trimmed to have a flat base, cover with orange fondant

2. Prepare cake pieces for decoration, following instructions in Sections A–D on pages 26–31.

3. On the iced cake board, use a toothpick to score lines where the railway track will be laid.

4. Assemble railway track.

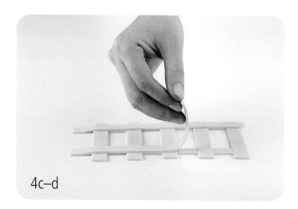

4c–d

    a. Roll out ivory fondant until about 2 mm ($^1/_8$ in) thick.

    b. Form the horizontal railway ties. Using a ruler and blade tool, cut out strips, each 1.5 cm ($^3/_4$ in) wide and about 8 cm (3 in) long. Lightly brush one side of each strip with water and attach to the cake board according to the scored markings.

c. Form support for the parallel rails. Cut out a long strip of fondant with a 3 mm ($^1/_8$ in) width. Trim the strip into short lengths to fit into the gap between each railway tie. Brush one side of each strip with water and attach between adjacent railway tie gaps.

d. Form the two parallel rails. Using a ruler and blade tool, cut out two strips of fondant, each 5 mm ($^1/_4$ in) wide. Lightly brush one side of each strip with water and overlay the railway ties and support to complete the railway track.

5. Form the train chimney.

a. Roll blue fondant into a ball. Shape into a cylindrical shape with a wide top by moving palms in opposite directions. Trim the narrower end to get a flat surface.

b. Insert a toothpick into the trimmed end for attaching onto the train later.

c. Wrap two thin white strips of fondant around the chimney, securing them with light brushes of water.

6. Create star trails.

a. Roll out fondant of various colours until about 2 mm ($^1/_8$ in) thick. Press star-shape cutters onto fondant sheets to cut out several stars.

b. Dampen one end of a wire and insert into a star. Repeat until there are enough to decorate the back of the train.

7. Form flowers. Roll out flower paste of various colours until about 2 mm ($^1/_8$ in) thick. Press flower cutters onto flower paste to cut out flowers. Leave flowers to set in a flower setter or painter's palette. Pipe green royal icing onto flower centres. Leave to dry overnight.

8. Assemble train wheels.

8a–d

    a. Roll out a thick layer of black fondant and press out wheels with a round cutter.

    b. Roll out purple fondant thinly and cut out rounds with a smaller round cutter.

    c. For the yellow star, roll out yellow fondant thinly. Press a star-shape cutter onto yellow fondant to cut out several stars.

    d. Assemble each wheel as shown using light brushes of water. Pipe beads of yellow royal icing all around.

9. Attach black borders on train. Roll out black fondant thinly. Trim into strips and attach to the bottom of the train with light brushes of water.

10. Attach purple stripes on train. Roll out purple fondant thinly. Trim into strips and attach to each compartment with light brushes of water.

11. Attach red roof. Roll out red fondant until about 5 mm ($^1/_4$ in) thick. Cut out a rectangle with a ruler and blade tool. Attach to the green compartment with a light brush of water.

12. Form fondant pieces for the hair and features as shown. Attach to the face with light brushes of water. For the eyes and blushes, press to flatten slightly. Mix charcoal dust with liquor or water. Paint the eyes. Attach the face to the front of the carriage with light brushes of water.

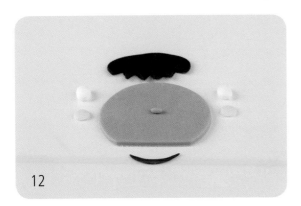

13. Form headlights. Roll blue and white fondant separately into balls, then press a ball of white fondant onto a ball of blue fondant. Repeat to make the other headlight. Attach to the front of the carriage with light brushes of water.

14. Assemble the train.

   a. Assemble the train tiers by following the instructions in Section E on pages 32–33.

   b. Insert train chimney that was made earlier.

   c. Decorate as desired, with flowers and star trails or pipe decorative patterns using royal icing.

   d. Shape black, grey and brown fondant into irregular shapes to resemble pebbles and stones. Attach to cake board as decoration with light brushes of water.

Dainty Cat on Pillow

Equipment

- Serrated knife
- Paintbrush
- Black satin ribbon
- Purple satin ribbon
- Craft glue or hot glue
- Rolling pin
- Ruler
- Blade tool
- Serrated tracing wheel
- Toothpick

Ingredients

- Single-tiered square cake
- Fondant — yellow, white, grey, brown, pink
- Water for brushing
- Royal icing
- Edible dust — charcoal
- Clear liquor or water for painting

METHOD

1. Chill cake for 30–45 minutes to aid trimming.

2. Trim cake into a pillow shape.

a. Trim cake to get a flat surface, then turn it so that its underside faces up.

b. Cut a curve on each side. Flip cake over and trim in the same manner.

c. Trim to soften the curved edges on all sides.

3. Prepare for decoration, following instructions in Sections A–D on pages 26–31.

   a. For this cake, the yellow fondant should be applied in two separate sheets. Cover the top surface first, giving enough allowance for the fondant sheet to drape over the edges. Flip to the other side and cover with another fondant sheet of the same size. Seal the joints at the sides with some water. To hide the seam, roll out a spaghetti-thin string of fondant and attach to the joint with a light brush of water.

   b. Decorate cake board by adhering black satin ribbon to the side with glue. Overlay with a thinner purple ribbon, securing it with glue.

4. Create white trimmings.

4a

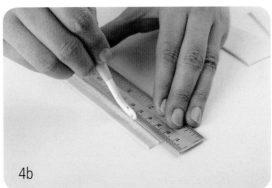

4b

4c

a. Roll out white fondant thinly. Trim into a rectangular sheet before cutting out zigzag patterns. Brush one side with water and attach to the cake.

b. Roll out grey fondant thinly. Use a ruler and a serrated tracing wheel to cut out lengthy strips of wavy lace. To create a dotted sewing line, lightly run the serrated tracing wheel down the middle of each strip. Be careful not to cut through the strip.

c. Brush one side with water and attach as a border to the white trimmings.

5. Assemble the cat.

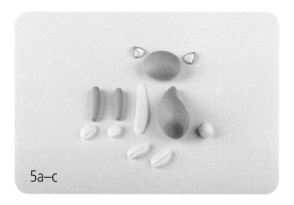

5a–c   5d

a. Shape the different parts of the cat as shown. Start every piece by rolling the fondant into a round ball, then mould with both palms moving in opposite directions to get the desired shapes.

b. Use a blade tool to impress lines on the paws.

c. For the ears, roll white and brown fondant balls separately. The white balls should be slightly smaller than the brown ones. Press each white fondant ball onto the brown one, then shape until it resembles pointed cat ears.

d. Attach a small thin sheet of white fondant to the cat's face with a light brush of water.

e. Insert a toothpick down the centre of the cat's neck. Press the head down the toothpick to attach it to the body.

f. Insert another toothpick into the centre of the base of the cat. Leave part of the toothpick exposed for inserting into the cake.

g. Adhere legs with light brushes of water. Note that the hind paws are longer than the front paws.

6. Mix charcoal dust with liquor or water. Paint the cat's face.

7. Make a ribbon rose for the cat using pink fondant.
   See Steps 6a–c on page 84.

8. Attach the cat to the cake with royal icing.

Jungle Safari

Equipment

- Serrated knife
- Red satin ribbon
- Orange satin ribbon
- Craft glue or hot glue
- Rolling pin
- Ruler
- Blade tool
- Separate paintbrushes for dry and wet applications
- Round cutters of two different sizes
- Rotary cutter
- Foam pad
- Leaf-shaper tool
- Toothpicks
- Lollipop sticks

Ingredients

- Two round cakes of the same circumference
- Fondant — various colours
- Flower paste — white
- Water for brushing
- Edible dust — charcoal, pink
- Clear liquor or water for painting
- Royal icing

METHOD

1. Chill cakes for 30–45 minutes to aid trimming.

2. Stack the cakes.

a. Trim the bottom tier to taper it all around.

b. Trim all around to get an even surface.

3. Prepare for decoration, following instructions in Sections A–D on pages 26–31.

a. Stack and coat the cakes together, there is no need for dowelling.

b. Use dark green fondant to cover the cake.

c. Decorate the cake board by adhering red satin ribbon. Overlay with a thinner orange satin ribbon, securing it with glue.

4. Form the rainbow.

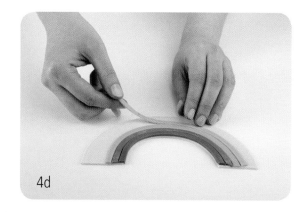

a. Prepare a template for the rainbow. Roll out white flower paste until about 2 mm ($^1/_8$ in) thick. Trim into a rainbow arch. Note that the arch must be wide enough to accommodate seven strips of colours. Leave to dry overnight.

b. Roll out fondant of the various rainbow colours thinly.

c. Using a ruler and blade tool, cut thin strips of each colour, each about 5 mm ($^3/_4$ in) thick.

d. Brush one side of each strip with water and attach directly onto the rainbow template. Leave to set.

5. Form letter tags.

a. Roll out fondant of various colours separately into thin sheets. Press round cutters onto fondant sheets to cut out two different sizes of fondant rounds. Attach smaller rounds to bigger rounds with light brushes of water. Make as many tags as required.

b. Mix charcoal dust with liquor or water. Paint letters onto the tags.

c. Using light brushes of water or royal icing, attach letter tags onto the cake.

6. Form leaves.

6c

a. Roll out light green and dark green fondant separately until about 2 mm ($^1/_8$ in) thick.

b. Using a rotary cutter, cut out leaf shapes of various sizes.

c. On a foam pad, use a leaf-shaper tool to impress lines that resemble veins.

d. Attach leaves to the cake with light brushes of water.

7. Assemble the lion.

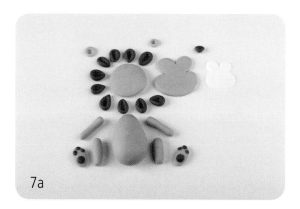

7a

a. Shape the different parts of the lion as shown. Start every piece by rolling the fondant into a round ball, then mould with both palms moving in opposite directions to get the desired shapes.

b. For the mane, roll small beads of dark brown fondant into a ball. Use a leaf-shaper tool to dent the centre of each bead.

c. For the eyes, press a small bead of blue fondant onto a small white ball. Repeat to make the other eye.

d. Assemble the head by adhering the various pieces with light brushes of water.

e. For the paws, press small beads of dark brown fondant into lighter brown balls.

f. Attach the body onto the cake with royal icing. Insert a toothpick down the centre of the body, leaving half of it exposed to attach the head.

g. Attach the legs to the body with light brushes of water.

h. Mix charcoal dust with liquor or water and paint the lion's features. Use a dry brush to apply pink dust for the blush.

8. Assemble the elephant.

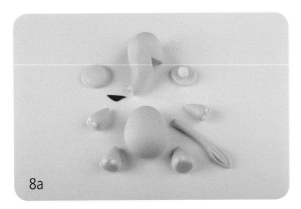

8a

a. Shape the different parts of the elephant as shown. Start every piece by rolling the fondant into a round ball, then mould with both palms moving in opposite directions to get the desired shapes.

b. For the head and trunk, shape into a large curved cylinder, then use a blade tool to cut a V opening for the mouth.

c. For the tongue, shape a thin sheet of red fondant into a triangle. Attach the tongue to the mouth with a light brush of water.

d. For the ears, press each ball of pink fondant onto the grey one.

e. For the legs, press small beads of white fondant onto grey balls.

f. For the eyes, press a small bead of blue fondant onto a small white ball. Repeat to make the other eye.

g. Attach the body onto the cake with royal icing. Insert a toothpick down the centre of the body, leaving half of it exposed to attach the head.

h. Join the remaining pieces to the body with light brushes of water.

9. Assemble the cake.

a. Position rainbow on the cake. Behind each end of the rainbow, insert two lollipop sticks into the cake, leaving two-thirds exposed to prop up the rainbow. The rainbow will rest against the lollipop sticks for support. To further secure the rainbow, use royal icing to attach the rainbow to the lollipop sticks.

b. Mix charcoal dust with liquor or water and highlight the eyes. Using a dry paintbrush, apply pink dust to the bridge of the trunk.

Grassy Meadow in Spring

Equipment

- Serrated knife
- Red satin ribbon
- Craft glue or hot glue
- Rolling pin
- Rotary cutter
- Serrated tracing wheel
- Paintbrush
- Piping bag and piping tip
- Ruler
- Blade tool
- Ball tool
- Gold wire

Ingredients

- Single-tiered round cake
- Fondant — green, sky blue, black, white, grey, red, light grey
- Water for brushing
- Royal icing — dark green
- Flower paste — yellow
- Edible lustre dust — silver
- Clear liquor or water for painting
- Brown sugar
- Transparent piping jelly

METHOD

1. Trim cake.

   a. Trim off uneven surface and the sharp edge until it is more rounded. Retain the dome shape of the cake.

   b. Create an uneven surface on a small portion of the cake for the lake.

2. Prepare for decoration, following instructions in Sections A–D on pages 26–31.

   a. Use green fondant to cover the cake.

   b. Decorate the cake board by adhering red satin ribbon to the side with glue.

3. Create the lake and sand compound.

   a. Roll out sky blue fondant until about 2 mm ($^1/_8$ in) thick. Using a rotary cutter, trim out an irregular shape and apply to the dented area on the cake with a light brush of water.

   b. Pipe dark green royal icing all around the lake and sand compound to resemble grass.

4. Assemble golf bag.

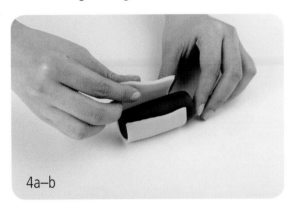

4a–b

4c

   a. Roll out yellow flower paste until about 2 mm ($^1/_8$ in) thick. With the help of a ruler and a blade tool, trim out a 9 x 15 cm ($3^1/_2$ x 6 in) rectangular sheet.

   b. Roll black fondant into a ball, then lengthen into a cylinder about 16 cm ($6^1/_2$ in) long. Flatten both ends. Wrap yellow bag cover over it and let it overlap a little. Trim off excess and brush the overlapping portion with a bit of water to seal. Leave one end of the black fondant exposed.

   c. Create designs. Roll out strips of black and red fondant separately until about 3 mm ($^1/_8$ in) thick. Trim into strips using a ruler and a serrated tracing wheel.

d. Attach to the bag with light brushes of water.

e. Roll light grey fondant into several elliptical discs. Use a blade tool to impress lines on each of them to resemble a golf clubhead. Dampen the ends of toothpicks and insert into each clubhead.

f. For the golf club handle, wrap black fondant around the top of the other end.

g. When the fondant has dried, mix silver lustre dust with liquor or water. Paint the golf shafts, clubheads and a decorative strip on the golf bag silver.

h. Insert a few golf clubs into the bag.

5. Assemble the cake.

a. Attach golf bag and golf club onto the cake with royal icing.

b. Form golf balls. Roll small balls of white fondant. Use a ball tool to create dents on each ball. Attach to the cake with light brushes of water.

c. Pipe green royal icing around the cake to resemble patches of grass.

d. Fill the sand compound with brown sugar.

e. Cut out a triangular piece of red fondant for the flag. Dampen one end of a gold wire and insert it into the red fondant. Insert flag near the sand compound.

6. Just before serving, fill the lake with piping jelly to resemble ripples of water.

At the Movies

Equipment

- Rolling pin
- Round cutters of various sizes
- Paintbrush
- Serrated knife
- Star-shape cutter
- Ball tool
- Ruler
- Blade tool
- Piping bag
- Black satin ribbon
- Craft glue or hot glue
- Lollipop stick

Ingredients

- Flower paste — grey
- Edible lustre dust — silver
- Clear liquor or water for painting
- One square cake + two round cakes of the same size
- Fondant — white, red, yellow, black
- Water for brushing
- Edible dust — yellow, brown
- Royal icing

METHOD

1. Create film roll casings.

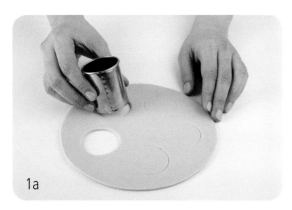

1a

   a. Roll out grey flower paste thinly for the film roll casings. Cut out four round pieces, with a diameter of about 2 cm ($^4/_5$ in) wider than that of each cake. For the top casing, cut out five holes with a round cutter. Leave to dry overnight.

   b. Mix silver lustre dust with liquor or water. Paint the casings silver and leave to dry.

2. Assemble the popcorn bag.

2a

2b

2f

2h

a. Trim a square cake into the shape of a popcorn bag, slicing away uneven surfaces. Trim the bottom so that it tapers.

b. Trim cake into a trapezium.

c. Prepare popcorn bag cake for decoration. See instructions in Sections A–D on pages 26–31. Wrap the fondant such that the joints are hidden beneath the cake.

d. To decorate the popcorn bag, roll out white fondant thinly. Cut thin strips to adhere to the popcorn bag with light brushes of water.

e. For the decorative star label, cut out a red star fondant and a round white fondant. Attach to the popcorn bag with light brushes of water.

f. For the popcorn, roll light yellow fondant into irregular pieces. Use a ball tool to create dents on each piece to resemble popcorn.

g. Mix yellow dust with liquor or water. Dab onto popcorn randomly.

h. Mix brown dust with liquor or water. Dab onto popcorn randomly to resemble caramelised portions.

3. Assemble the clapperboard.

a. Roll out black fondant until about 3 mm ($^1/_8$ in) thick. Using a ruler and a blade tool, cut out the shape of a clapperboard. Leave to dry.

b. Roll out white fondant thinly. Cut into long strips, each 0.5 cm ($^1/_4$ in) wide. Adhere to the clapperboard with light brushes of water.

c. Cut out more strips, each 1.5 cm ($^3/_4$ in) wide. Adhere these to border the lid of the clapperboard.

d. Pipe royal icing onto the clapperboard to personalise a message.

4. Assemble film rolls.

4c–d

a. Prepare two round cakes for decoration, following instructions in Sections A–D on pages 26–31. Use chocolate ganache for filling and coating cakes.

b. Roll out white fondant thinly. Trim into two long strips, each the length of the circumference of a cake, and as wide as the height of the cake.

c. Roll out black fondant thinly. Cut into four long thin strips, each the same length as the white strips above. Attach to the top and bottom edge of each white strip with light brushes of water.

d. Cut out shorter black strips to attach between the parallel black strips.

e. Attach to the sides of the round cakes so that they resemble film rolls.

5. Assemble cake tiers. See instructions in Section E on pages 32–33.

a. Decorate cake board by adhering black satin ribbon to the side with glue.

b. Attach one film roll casing to the iced cake board with light brushes of water, where the bottom tier will be placed. Assemble cake tiers using chocolate ganache.

c. Sandwich each cake tier with film roll casings.

6. Do up the final touches.

    a. Attach popcorn bag to the cake board with royal icing. Loosely arrange popcorn spilling out of the bag.

    b. Insert a lollipop stick on top of the cake as a support for the clapperboard. Secure the clapperboard to the lollipop stick with royal icing.

    c. Make as many red stars as desired to decorate cake board. For the star décor, see Step 6 on page 123.

Sweet Pink Bag

Equipment

- Serrated knife
- Rolling pin
- Ruler
- Blade tool
- Paintbrush
- Cone tool
- Serrated tracing wheel
- Alphabet cutters

Ingredients

- One square cake
- Fondant — baby pink, deep pink, various colours as desired
- Water for brushing
- Flower paste — baby pink (optional)
- Royal icing

METHOD

1. Trim a square cake into the shape of a bag.

2. Prepare for decoration, following instructions in Sections A–D on pages 26–31.

    a. Use pink fondant to cover the cake.

3. Form the zip.

    a. Roll out deep pink fondant until about 3 mm ($^1/_8$ in) thick. Using a ruler and blade tool, trim out a strip slightly longer than the top of the bag. Impress lines onto the strip to resemble a zip.

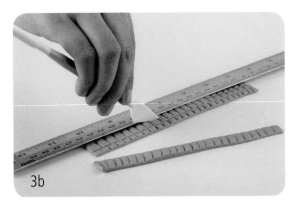 

b. Trim until zip is of a desired width.

c. Lightly brush the underside of the zip with water and attach to the top of the bag.

d. For the zip handle, mould deep pink fondant into a teardrop shape. Lightly press to flatten slightly. Use a cone tool to form a hole through the rounded end. Attach to one end of the zip with a light brush of water.

4. Form bag handles.

a. Roll out baby pink fondant thinly. Trim into two long strips of desired width and length.

b. Brush both sides of each strip with water. Shape handles as desired and leave to set. When dry, attach to the bag with royal icing. If you wish to have stiffer standing handles, use flower paste instead.

5. Create bag design.

a. Roll out deep pink and baby pink fondant separately into two thin sheets. Cut into rectangular panels.

b. Attach the panels in alternate colours onto the bottom of the bag with light brushes of water.

6. Form pleats.

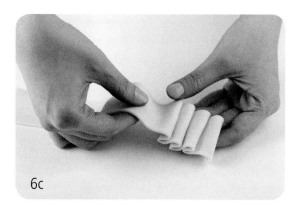

6c

a. Roll out baby pink fondant thinly. Cut into a 3 cm (1¹/₄ in) wide strip, and long enough to form pleats all around the bag.

b. With the help of a ruler, run a serrated tracing wheel along both sides of the strip to resemble sewing lines.

c. Hold one end of the strip and fold lightly to form a pleat. Brush the back of the fold with a little water and press gently to secure the pleated fold. Repeat until the pleated strip is long enough to encircle the bag. Attach to the bag with royal icing.

7. Cut out fondant letters of different colours with alphabet cutters. Attach to the cake with light brushes of water.

Templates

These templates can be photocopied for use in decorating projects. Increase or decrease the size of each template as desired.

CAKE AND ICING RECIPES

Chocolate Cake

Yields one 15-cm (6-in) round cake + one 22.5-cm (9-in) round cake, each 5 cm (2 in) in height

Cake flour 500 g (1 lb 1$^1/_2$ oz)

Baking powder 1 Tbsp + 1 tsp

Salt 1 tsp

Baking chocolate 454 g (1 lb),
    finely chopped

Butter 227 g (8 oz)

Fine sugar 365 g (12$^3/_4$ oz)

Eggs 4

Vanilla extract 2 tsp

Milk 334 ml (11$^1/_3$ fl oz)

1. Preheat oven to 176°C (349°F). Grease cake pan and line with parchment paper.

2. Sift flour, baking powder and salt together. Set aside.

3. Melt chocolate over simmering water in a heat-resistant bowl. Set aside.

4. Cream butter until light and fluffy.

5. Add sugar and beat well.

6. Add one egg at a time, beating well before adding the next one.

7. Add melted chocolate and beat well, then add vanilla extract and continue to mix.

8. Add sifted dry ingredients and milk in batches. Alternate their additions, starting and ending with the dry ingredients, all the while beating to mix well.

9. Pour batter into cake pan. Bake for about 45 minutes for a 15-cm (6-in) round cake, and 50–60 minutes for a 22.5-cm (9-in) round cake. Note that baking times will vary across different ovens.

10. When the baking time is almost up, test doneness by inserting a cake tester into the centre of the cake. Cake is done if the tester comes out clean.

11. Leave to cool for about 15 minutes before removing the cake from the pan. Leave cake to cool completely on a wire rack before using.

Butter Cake

Yields two 15-cm (6-in) round cakes OR a 22.5-cm (9-in) round cake, each 5 cm (2 in) in height

Cake flour 260 g (9 oz)

Salt $1/2$ tsp

Baking powder 4 tsp

Vegetable shortening 149 g (5$1/3$ oz)

Fine sugar 160 g (5$2/3$ oz) + 60 g (2 oz)

Milk 240 ml (8 fl oz / 1 cup)

Egg white from 4 eggs

1. Preheat oven to 160°C (325°F). Grease cake pan and line with parchment paper.

2. Sift flour, salt and baking powder together.

3. Cream shortening until light.

4. Add 160 g (5$2/3$ oz) sugar to shortening. Beat to combine.

5. Add sifted dry ingredients and milk to shortening mixture in batches. Alternate their additions, starting and ending with the dry ingredients, all the while beating to mix well.

6. Beat egg white with 60 g (2 oz) fine sugar until stiff and shiny. Fold into batter until well combined.

7. Pour batter into cake pan. Bake for about 45 minutes for a 15-cm (6-in) round cake, and 50–60 minutes for a 22.5-cm (9-in) round cake. Note that baking times will vary across different ovens.

8. When the baking time is almost up, test doneness by inserting a cake tester into the centre of the cake. Cake is done if the tester comes out clean.

9. Leave to cool for about 15 minutes before removing the cake from the pan. Leave cake to cool completely on a wire rack before using.

Butter Cake Variations

Butter Cake Flavour	Flavouring Ingredients	Notes
Vanilla	**Vanilla seeds** from $\frac{1}{2}$ pod OR **Vanilla essence** 2 tsp	
Pandan	**Pandan essence** 2 tsp OR Substitute 2 Tbsp milk with 2 Tbsp fresh pandan juice	
Lavender	**Lavender essence** 2 tsp OR **Lavender flowers** 8 g ($\frac{1}{3}$ oz)	
Lemon	**Lemon zest** from 4 lemons **Lemon juice** 40 ml ($1\frac{2}{5}$ fl oz) **Lemon flavouring** 1 tsp	
Chocolate Marble	**Premium grade dark chocolate** 80 g ($2\frac{4}{5}$ oz), melted via a bain marie	Swirl into batter in small batches to create a marbling effect.

Oreo Butter Cake

Yields one 15-cm (6-in) round cake + one 22.5-cm (9-in) round cake, each 5 cm (2 in) in height

Vegetable shortening 149 g
(5^1/$_3$ oz)

Fine sugar 140 g (5 oz) +
80 g (2^4/$_5$ oz)

Cake flour 230 g (8^1/$_4$ oz)

Salt ^{1}/$_2$ tsp

Baking powder 4 tsp

Milk 190 ml (6^1/$_2$ fl oz)

Egg white from 5 eggs

Cream cheese 150 g (5^1/$_3$ oz)

Oreo cookies 60 g (2 oz), cream
removed

1. Preheat oven to 160°C (325°F). Grease cake pan and line with parchment paper.

2. Cream shortening, then add 140 g (5 oz) sugar.

3. Sift cake flour, salt and baking powder together.

4. While beating the shortening mixture, add in flour mixture and milk separately. Alternate the additions of dry and wet ingredients, beginning and ending with dry ingredients.

5. Add cream cheese.

6. Beat egg white and 80 g (2^4/$_5$ oz) sugar together. Fold into batter.

7. Pour batter into cake pan. Bake for about 45 minutes for a 15-cm (6-in) round cake, and 50–60 minutes for a 22.5-cm (9-in) round cake. Note that baking times will vary across different ovens.

8. When the baking time is almost up, test doneness by inserting a cake tester into the centre of the cake. Cake is done if the tester comes out clean.

9. Leave to cool for about 15 minutes before removing the cake from the pan. Leave cake to cool completely on a wire rack before using.

Note: Oreo butter cake pairs well with Oreo mint buttercream.

Buttercreams

Yields enough for filling and coating three 22.5-cm (9-in) round cakes, each 5 cm (2 in) in height

Egg white 135 g (4²/₃ oz)

Icing sugar 270 g (9¹/₂ oz)

Unsalted butter 510 g
(1 lb ¹/₃ oz)

Shortening 150 g (5¹/₃ oz)

Flavouring (if using) see table
below

1. Beat egg white, then add icing sugar in three batches, beating along the way until well incorporated before adding the next batch.

2. Heat egg white mixture via a bain marie at 70–80°C (158–176°K). Beat until it foams.

3. Remove from heat. Continue to beat until stiff peaks form.

4. Add butter gradually in batches, mixing well along the way until well incorporated before adding the next batch.

5. Add shortening and beat until well incorporated.

6. Add desired flavouring, if using, and mix well. Buttercream is now ready for use.

Buttercream Flavour	Flavouring Ingredients	Notes
Vanilla	**Vanilla pod** 1 OR **Vanilla essence** 2 tsp	
Chocolate	**Chocolate ganache** (see page 168)	• Ratio of chocolate ganache to buttercream is 1:1
Earl Grey Lavender	**Water** 150 ml (5 fl oz) **Earl Grey tea leaves** 7 g (¹/₃ oz) **Lavender flowers** 4 g (¹/₅ oz) Sugar 2 Tbsp	• Heat all ingredients together and leave to reduce until one-third is left. • Add 2 Tbsp to every 200 g (7 oz) buttercream.
Lemon Rose	**Rose flavouring** ¹/₄ tsp **Lemon juice** 1 Tbsp	• Add to every 150 g (5¹/₃ oz) buttercream
Coconut	**Desiccated coconut** 20 g (²/₃ oz), baked	• Add to every 200 g (7 oz) buttercream.
Oreo Mint	**Mint paste** ¹/₂ tsp	• Add to every 50 g (1²/₃ oz) buttercream.

Chocolate Ganache

Yields about 1 kg (2 lb 3 oz) chocolate ganache

Premium grade dark chocolate 500 g (1 lb, 1¹/₂ oz), chopped

Double (heavy) cream 500 ml (16 fl oz / 2 cups)

1. Place chocolate in a heat-resistant bowl.

2. Heat cream in a saucepan over medium heat until it just reaches a boil. Remove from heat immediately and pour over the chocolate.

3. Stir gently to completely cover chocolate with cream. Continue to stir in one direction until smooth and well blended.

4. Leave to cool before using or refrigerating.

Decorative Icing: Royal Icing

Yield depends on quantity of egg white

Egg white from 2 eggs
Cream of tartar 1/2 tsp
Water 1 tsp
Icing (confectioner's) sugar as needed, sifted to prevent clumping
Desired flavouring (if using) 1/2 tsp

1. Pour egg white, cream of tartar and water into a mixing bowl. Beat until foamy.

2. Beat in 1 Tbsp icing sugar. Once icing sugar starts to get incorporated, gradually beat in more to achieve desired consistency. Stop adding icing sugar when desired consistency is achieved. Note that the more icing sugar is added, the stiffer the royal icing.

3. Add desired flavouring if using. Mix well.

   a. Stiff consistency: can hold a firm peak, and is suitable for piping decorations such as flowers and ruffles

   b. Medium consistency: able to hold a soft peak, and is suitable for attaching decorations to cakes, as well as piping texts and borders

   c. Flood consistency: runny, and is suitable for coating surfaces

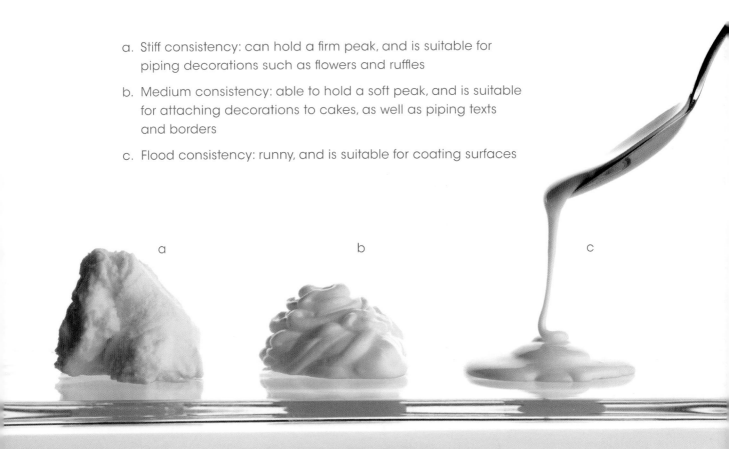

a   b   c

Decorative Icing: Fondant

Yields about 1 kg (2 lb 3 oz) fondant

Unflavoured gelatin powder
  1 Tbsp

Cold water 57 ml (2 fl oz)

Glucose 170 g (6 oz)

Glycerin 1$^1/_2$ Tbsp

Flavouring or colouring (if using)
  1 tsp

Icing sugar 880 g (1 lb 15 oz),
  sifted (adjust according to
  desired consistency)

1. Sprinkle gelatin powder into water. Leave to bloom for 5 minutes.

2. Heat bloomed gelatin via a bain marie until it is clear. Do not boil.

3. Remove from heat and add glucose and glycerin. Stir well.

4. Add flavouring or colouring if using. Mix well.

5. Pour into a mixing bowl. Knead in icing sugar until desired consistency is achieved.

6. Shape into a ball and wrap tightly in cling film. Store in an airtight container. Allow to rest at room temperature for about 8 hours before using, especially if the weather is humid. Do not refrigerate. Note that an iced cake should not be refrigerated as condensation may form on the fondant surface when taken out of the refrigerator after some time.

Suggestions:

500 g (1 lb 1$^1/_2$ oz) covers a 15-cm (6-in) round cake

680 g (1$^1/_2$ lb) covers a 20-cm (8-in) round cake

1 kg (2 lb 3 oz) covers a 25-cm (10-in) round cake

1 kg 400 g (3 lb) covers a 30-cm (12-in) round cake

Note that the each of the cakes is 10 cm (4 in) in height.

Decorative Icing: Flower Paste

Yields about 600 g (1 lb 5²/₅ oz) flower paste

Gelatin powder 6 g (²/₃ oz)
Cold water 25 ml (⁴/₅ fl oz)
Glucose 16 g (¹/₂ oz)
Shortening 15 g (¹/₂ oz)
Icing sugar 500 g (1 lb 1¹/₂ oz)
Tylose powder 1 tsp
Egg white from 1 egg

1. Sprinkle gelatin powder into water. Leave to bloom.

2. Heat bloomed gelatin via a bain marie until it is clear. Do not boil.

3. Remove from heat. Stir in glucose and shortening. Mix well.

4. Sift icing sugar into a mixing bowl. Add tylose powder.

5. Pour in egg white and beat to mix well.

6. Knead thoroughly and store tightly wrapped in cling film at room temperature.

Colour Tinting

1. Gel colourings are recommended for tinting fondant or flower paste.

2. Start by adding a small quantity of colouring, then knead fondant or flower paste to distribute colours evenly. Continue to add colouring and knead until the desired colour or shade is achieved.

3. It is possible to mix different colours of fondant or flower paste to achieve a secondary colour, e.g. pink + orange = peach.

4. When mixing dark colours, use food-safe gloves to avoid staining your hands.

5. To tint a big batch of fondant, always start by mixing a small quantity of fondant with concentrated gel colouring first. Knead to distribute the colour evenly before kneading with a larger piece of fondant. Knead until the colour is evenly distributed.

6. Sunlight will cause some colours to fade. After the cake is decorated, it is best to store in a cool room and out of direct sunlight.

7. Deep colours like red and black may cause a bitter aftertaste. Look out for colourings that indicate "no taste" on the labels.

General Notes

1. When baking cakes, all ingredients should be at room temperature.

2. While both fondant and flower paste can be used for making cake decorations, each of them have different properties. It is therefore important to take note of the following before deciding which one to use for your decorations.

    a. Flower paste is hard and brittle when dry, making it messy and difficult to cut through, especially if it covers an area on the cake that needs to be cut. Fondant, on the other hand, remains soft even after it has set, making it easier to cut through without making a mess.

    b. Whenever a decorative item needs to stand upright, or when it needs to retain its shape, flower paste instead of fondant is used since it is firmer when dried.

3. Dust moulds or cutters with icing (confectioner's) sugar or corn flour (cornstarch) before use. This will make removing the fondant or flower paste easier. If you would like to add a shimmer, use pearl dust instead.

4. Before painting, mix edible dust with clear liquor or water. Water works as well as liquor, except that liquor dries faster.

5. To secure heavier items, use royal icing instead of water, as royal icing will harden when dry, making the items more secure.

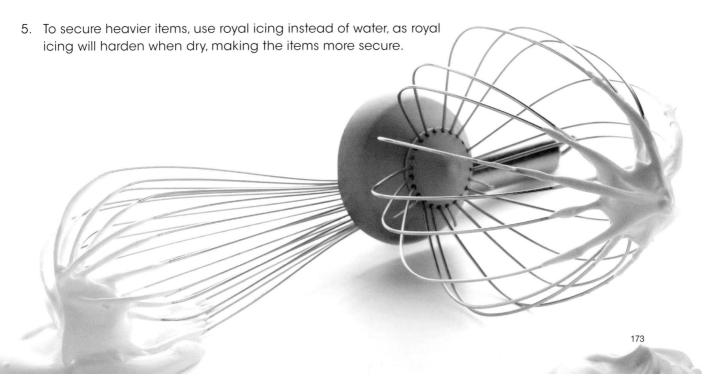

Weights and Measures

Quantities for this book are given in Metric and American (spoon and cup) measures. Standard spoon and cup measurements used are: 1 tsp = 5 ml, 1 Tbsp = 15 ml, 1 cup = 250 ml. All measures are level unless otherwise stated.

LIQUID AND VOLUME MEASURES

Metric	Imperial	American
5 ml	$^1/_6$ fl oz	1 tsp
10 ml	$^1/_3$ fl oz	1 dsp
15 ml	$^1/_2$ fl oz	1 Tbsp
60 ml	2 fl oz	$^1/_4$ cup (4 Tbsp)
85 ml	2 $^1/_2$ fl oz	$^1/_3$ cup
90 ml	3 fl oz	$^3/_8$ cup (6 Tbsp)
125 ml	4 fl oz	$^1/_2$ cup
180 ml	6 fl oz	$^3/_4$ cup
250 ml	8 fl oz	1 cup
300 ml	10 fl oz ($^1/_2$ pint)	1$^1/_4$ cups
375 ml	12 fl oz	1$^1/_2$ cups
435 ml	14 fl oz	1$^3/_4$ cups
500 ml	16 fl oz	2 cups
625 ml	20 fl oz (1 pint)	2$^1/_2$ cups
750 ml	24 fl oz (1$^1/_5$ pints)	3 cups
1 litre	32 fl oz (1$^3/_5$ pints)	4 cups
1.25 litres	40 fl oz (2 pints)	5 cups
1.5 litres	48 fl oz (2$^2/_5$ pints)	6 cups
2.5 litres	80 fl oz (4 pints)	10 cups

DRY MEASURES

Metric	Imperial
30 grams	1 ounce
45 grams	1$^1/_2$ ounces
55 grams	2 ounces
70 grams	2$^1/_2$ ounces
85 grams	3 ounces
100 grams	3$^1/_2$ ounces
110 grams	4 ounces
125 grams	4$^1/_2$ ounces
140 grams	5 ounces
280 grams	10 ounces
450 grams	16 ounces (1 pound)
500 grams	1 pound, 1$^1/_2$ ounces
700 grams	1$^1/_2$ pounds
800 grams	1$^1/_2$ pounds
1 kilogram	2 pounds, 3 ounces
1.5 kilograms	3 pounds, 4$^1/_2$ ounces
2 kilograms	4 pounds, 6 ounces

OVEN TEMPERATURE

	°C	°F	Gas Regulo
Very slow	120	250	1
Slow	150	300	2
Moderately slow	160	325	3
Moderate	180	350	4
Moderately hot	190/200	370/400	5/6
Hot	210/220	410/440	6/7
Very hot	230	450	8
Super hot	250/290	475/550	9/10

ABBREVIATION

tsp	teaspoon
Tbsp	tablespoon
g	gram
kg	kilogram
ml	millilitre

LENGTH

Metric	Imperial
0.5 cm	$^1/_4$ inch
1 cm	$^1/_2$ inch
1.5 cm	$^3/_4$ inch
2.5 cm	1 inch

Editor: Audrey Yow
Designer: Adithi Khandadi
Photographer: Liu Hongde, Hongde Photography

Published by Marshall Cavendish Cuisine
An imprint of Marshall Cavendish International
1 New Industrial Road, Singapore 536196

Other Marshall Cavendish Offices:
Marshall Cavendish Corporation. 99 White Plains Road, Tarrytown NY 10591-9001, USA • Marshall Cavendish International (Thailand) Co Ltd. 253 Asoke, 12th Flr, Sukhumvit 21 Road, Klongtoey Nua, Wattana, Bangkok 10110, Thailand • Marshall Cavendish (Malaysia) Sdn Bhd, Times Subang, Lot 46, Subang Hi-Tech Industrial Park, Batu Tiga, 40000 Shah Alam, Selangor Darul Ehsan, Malaysia

Marshall Cavendish is a trademark of Times Publishing Limited

National Library Board Singapore Cataloguing in Publication Data

Kok, Pei Shuen
Step-by-step Cake decorating with Cherylshuen. -- Singapore : Marshall Cavendish Cuisine, 2014.
pages cm
ISBN : 978-981-4398-09-1 (paperback)

1. Cake decorating. 2. Icings (Confectionary) I. Title.

TX771.2
641.86539-- dc23
OCN859837898

Printed in Singapore by KWF Printing Pte Ltd